# MOVING TO THE COUNTRY

After reading history at Oxford and cataloguing drawings and prints for Christie's, Huon Mallalieu became a full-time writer in 1973. He is the author of the standard reference book, *The Dictionary of British Watercolour Artists*, and has written or edited numerous works on art and antiques, including Boxtree's *Antiques Roadshow – A-Z of Antiques Hunting*. He has been a frequent contributor to *The Times* since 1976, and in 1990 was appointed saleroom writer for *Country Life*, one of the most prestigious jobs in the field. Wearing another hat, he won the 1998 award as Residential Property Journalist of the Year.

# MOVING TO THE COUNTRY

## A COUNTRY LIFE GUIDE

### Huon Mallalieu

BXTREE

First published in 2000 by Boxtree, an imprint of Macmillan Publishers Ltd,
25 Eccleston Place, London, SW1W 9NF
and Basingstoke

www.macmillan.co.uk

Associated companies throughout the world

ISBN 0 7522 1318 0

9 8 7 6 5 4 3 2 1

A CIP catalogue record for this book is available from the British Library

Cover photographs © Tony Stone Images.
Main photograph and inset (left): Charlie Waite. Inset (right) John Lawrence.
Maps supplied by ML Design, London
Typeset and designed by Blackjacks, London
Printed by Mackays of Chatham plc

*Country Life* is published by IPC Magazines Ltd, King's Reach Tower,
Stamford Street, London SE1 9LS. For subscription enquiries and overseas
orders call 01444 445555 (fax 01444 445599). Please send all correspondence
to: IPC Magazines Ltd, Oakfield House, 35 Perrymount Road, Haywards
Heath, West Sussex RH16 3DH. Alternatively, you can call the subscription
credit card hotline (UK orders only) on: 01622 778778.

# CONTENTS

# ACKNOWLEDGEMENTS

It would not have been possible to put this book together without mercilessly plundering the knowledge, experience and anecdotage of a wide network of friends and contacts. I am more grateful than I can express for the time and patience with which the following companies and individuals have greeted my demands.

## Agents and Companies
Bedfords, Bidwells, Blenkin & Blenkin, Browns, Carter Jonas, Cluttons Daniel Smith, Andrew Grant, Hayman-Joyce, Jackson-Stops & Staff, Knight Frank, Llewellyn Humphreys, Christopher Lyons, Mullocks-Wells, AXA Nordstern, FPDSavills, Strutt & Parker, John D.Wood

## Individuals
Rory & Fiona Annesley, Gilli Ardizzone, David Baldock, David Bedford, Alison Blease, Tim Blenkin, Sue Bond, Christopher Bosanquet, Richard Bowman, Dawn Christmas, Simon Clowes, Bill and Margie Coldrey, Delyth Davies, Charles Ellingworth, Jane Ewen, William Gething, Suzanne Goldklang, Andrew Grant, Alastair Hancock, Giles Harbottle, Bettina Harden, Peter Hale, Sarah Hale, James Hayman-Joyce, James Hayward, Nick and Serena Herbert, Nicholas Hextall, Ian Homersham, Malcolm Hornby, Carl Jackson-Plummer, Quentin Jackson-Stops, Guy Jenkinson, Henry Jones-Davis, Richard and Elaine Knight, Graham Knowles, Christopher Lacy, Martin Lamb, Lou Lidderdale, Camilla Lindsay, Jock Lloyd-Jones, Christopher Lyons, John Machin, Jonathan Major, Ann Mallalieu, Laura Mason, Trevor Masterson, Lee Menzies, Tony Morris-Eyton, Giles Mounsey-Heysham, Dixie Nicholls, Samantha Orde, Catherine Paice, Clare Pardy, Michael Parry-Jones, Henry Pryor, Julian Rowse, Rose Sanguinetti, Guy Schwinge, Clare Smith, Philippe Soulard, Mark Stewart, Roy Strong, John Vaughan, John White, Mary Wilson, Peter Young

## *Country Life* writers
Sue Corbett, Amicia de Moubray, Rachel Thomas, Rupert Uloth, Tony Venison

## Also at *Country Life*
Clive Aslet, Michael Hall, Hamish Dawson

And particularly my indefatigable researcher, Jodi Lawson, copy-editor Tessa Clark, my indomitable agent Caroline Davidson, and Emma Marriott, my unflustered editor at Boxtree.

# PREFACE

The countryside of England and Wales is one of the glories of the world. Very little of it is natural, in the sense of untouched by human hand; rather it is the triumphant result of nature and humanity working together. Chocolate boxes and tourist brochures may concentrate on thatch and blossom, but the real joy of the countryside lies in its variety. No two counties are truly alike, and within each there are differences of geography, character, building materials, weather and ways of life that mean that the people who live in the country are as various as itself.

One of the principal aims of this book is to celebrate that diversity, and so help people decide where they are likely to be happiest. All moves are stressful, but a move to the country may involve all sorts of extra twists and unexpected wrinkles, especially if it is to an area you do not really know well. I trust that some, at least, will be unravelled and smoothed over here.

People move out of cities into the country for many reasons, and their needs and expectations will not all be met in the same ways. I hope that this book, with a mixture of general advice and specific information, will prove useful both to end-to-end readers and to browsers and dippers. It is intended to help would-be movers of all types to make the right decisions for their circumstances, by highlighting factors which may not feature in agents' brochures. It brings together many of the sources of specialist advice and information that do exist, but do not always advertise themselves widely.

Obviously, it cannot provide all the answers for what is after all an all-encompassing business, but I hope that it will point the reader in the right directions and indicate some questions to answer, or at least consider, before making a move. Country life is a joy for very many people, but you must be sure that it will work for you. Quite often success is a matter of learning to think both positively and laterally.

What has been termed the 'crisis in the countryside' inevitably obtrudes at several points. There are many contentious issues, from massive house-building schemes and industrial development to organic farming, genetically modified crops, hunting and rights of way. You may feel that they have little to do with you, but we are witnessing something of a changing of the guard in the rural population, and the present generation of incomers will have a vital role in determining the future shape of the countryside. For this reason too, I have touched on relationships between incomers and established inhabitants, although social commentary is inevitably a minefield.

The chapters dealing with specific subjects are supplemented with county-by-county profiles, which contrast stereotypical – indeed caricature – images with reality, and wherever possible rely on local information. I have also included a directory that lists details of publications, sources of further advice and addresses of useful organizations and specialist firms.

# INTRODUCTION

B etween 1971 and 1991 the rural population of Britain rose by 17 per cent, while the population as a whole rose by only 4 per cent. This is remarkable because since at least the beginning of the eighteenth century, if not the mid-seventeenth, the principal movement of population in the British Isles was from the countryside into London and the other urban centres. The migration to the cities continued into the nineteenth century – the population of London rose from 864,845 to 1,873,676 between 1801 and 1841 – although the start of the century also saw a smaller counterflow of better-off citizens that resulted in the development of the first suburbs, with tasteful villas – mocked as 'cits' boxes' – crowding the hills north and south of London, and along the Thames at Richmond and Twickenham.

The remarkably rapid development of the railway system from the 1830s onwards accelerated this trend by making weekly and daily commuting practical. One of the cultural ironies of Victorian Britain is the way the new rich hung their Gothic and stockbrokers' Tudor country mansions in the Home Counties, Cheshire and similar new dormitories with paintings and watercolours celebrating the country cottages and rural ways of life they were destroying.

For most of the twentieth century the suburbs have devoured ever more of the countryside, and the relocation after the Second World War of large numbers of East Enders to Essex, Suffolk and towns such as High Wycombe usually augmented the populations of established urban centres rather than the true countryside. The subsequent establishment of Milton Keynes, Stevenage, Harlow and other new towns since the 1960s served to depopulate rural areas still further by creating new semi-urban magnets for those in search of work and subsidized housing.

Currently it is estimated that 1,700 people are moving to the country from Britain's cities every week. At the same time we are told of an increasing population seepage from the northern parts of England to the already crowded South-East. The reaction of planners, government advisers and, of course, the building and developing trades, is to propose ever increasing numbers of new houses, primarily in green belt and greenfield areas.

Although Surrey has long ceased to count as country for many people, it none the less still attracts toe-dippers from London, young couples deciding whether there really is life beyond the smoke. The same is true of those parts of Cheshire sometimes known as Manchester's Surrey. The South-West is ever popular with the retired and people planning for retirement. The Honiton office of the estate agent Humberts reported that in the summer months of 1999 they were selling between 60 and 70 per cent of the properties on their books to buyers from elsewhere, including people returning from abroad. Some of these will be buying holiday homes, or properties to be let until they wish to retire to them.

Even so, that 17 per cent rise in the rural population, and the reports that thousands are now deserting the cities month by month, are indeed startling. Some of the basic causes are obvious enough, including natural dissatisfaction with the grime of urban living and its cost, and worries about educational standards. However, increased freedom of mobility is perhaps the key, allied to the revolution in communications. No one now need stay where they happened to be born, unless they wish to, and fewer people are so tightly tied to a place of work. In a very positive way the new technology is making it considerably more practical, and pleasant, to work from a home in the country. Although the numbers of people who are already 'teleporting' may have been slightly exaggerated, the communications revolution is certainly playing a major part in changing the demography and character of the country – and the countryside. In the medium to long term it could well be the saving of rural life.

Moving to the country will be simplified by the development of Internet property selling, which enables potential buyers to obtain information quickly and easily. This is still in its infancy, but growth will be swift. On just one morning in early 1999 – probably a Monday, when Net business is briskest – Strutt & Parker's Exeter office noted enquiries from St Albans, Sweden, London and Kent.

In February 1999 the same agents, together with Gallup, undertook a survey to assess general attitudes to the countryside and aspects of the wider rural economy. The views of 1,000 British adults, from both town and country, were solicited by telephone. Questioned about the quality of life, 71 per cent believed it to be better in the countryside, although this fell to 60 per cent in the 16–24 age bracket. Of the urban sample, 66 per cent claimed that, given it were a practical option, they would happily move to the country. To accommodate this, 63 per cent would prefer to see a series of small housing developments rather than the building of large new towns.

## THE COUNTRY TODAY

In its invaluable discussion document on rural England, *Choose Livelihood*, the Countryside Alliance remembers to ask the most basic question of all: 'Where is the countryside?' For some people even Surrey still has its rural corners, but others would consider that there is no true countryside to be found anywhere in the South-East, which they see merely as a suburb of greater or lesser density.

While one perfectly reasonable but not particularly satisfactory answer might be 'in the mind of the beholder,' statistical definitions are scarcely more helpful. A standard European Union definition of rurality is based on a population of less than 100 people per square kilometre. This covers 11 per cent of the population of Great Britain. The complex definitions, including classifications of local and health authorities, used by the Office for National Statistics produce a similar, but surely too small, 10.8 per cent. However, for the Countryside Agency (see Directory, page 248), defining rurality by settlements of less than 10,000 people, 25 per cent of the English population is rural, which must err the other way. A widely accepted assertion is that five times more Britons live in cities than in the countryside. Perhaps the mind of the beholder is best after all.

At the time of writing the countryside, its problems and attractions, has become a hot subject in the newspapers. Hardly a day passes without discussion of the plight of hill farmers, abattoirs being closed down, the building of millions of houses, car accidents on country lanes, illnesses caused by pesticides or sheep dip, planning rows, inadequate bus services and the closure of village shops and schools – accompanied by surveys of either rural bliss or rural depression, depending on the editorial mood of the day.

Good and bad news is sometimes a matter of interpretation. On 21 July 1999 the *Independent* carried two stories about village life. Each seemed off-putting at first glance but on further reading will have upended many people's perceptions. The first concerned a report by researchers from Anglia University, Cambridge, into the behaviour of young people in Cambridgeshire villages. In particular they looked at the habit rural teenagers commonly have of hanging about, often at the village bus stop with its seats or shelter.

This could be intimidating for older residents but the researchers took a rather different view, which has its positive elements: 'Unlike teenagers in the towns, these young people have nothing to do. They are lucky if they get a youth club once a week. Because of poor public transport and services they feel trapped in their home villages. However, in turn they feel intimidated by the rest of the community. They are highly visible, are aware of their lack of anonymity and are concerned that their parents may be told of any bad behaviour. As a result they tend to be much more conformist'.

The second story hinged on the same point – the lack of anonymity in village life – and described a vicious poison-pen campaign that was being waged against a group of churchgoers in a Leicestershire village. The village is quite large, with about 5,000 inhabitants and many commuters, but it is still small enough for most people to know other people's business. As the vicar put it, 'In the country word soon gets round – whether you're up to no good, or whether you're in trouble and need help.' This may have been uncomfortable for the recipients of the letters, but could be of immense benefit for many more people in times of trouble.

In matters like these, village life does not alter much, but in other fundamental respects it does. We are in the middle of a period of change from which will emerge a country way of life very different to anything known by previous generations. The whole pattern of rural employment is changing, and this is a major component in increasing mobility of the population. It is probable that a new agricultural revolution will take place in the coming years.

This is likely to be on a par with the eighteenth-century agricultural and industrial revolutions, and a great many of its effects will be as positive. Somehow the pressures for large-scale 'agribusinesses' and the demands for sustainable and organic farming must be reconciled. Given these changes anyone moving to the country should be aware of what is happening now, because the present generation of incomers will have great influence on the future. A few years ago the move out of town could be made with little reference to farming methods, organic and genetic crops, working from home, planning and building policies, or even attitudes to blood sports. This is no longer the case.

It is not just that hedges have been grubbed out, and haystacks and corn stooks have long disappeared. You would probably have to be fifty to remember the stooks and soon, perhaps, younger people will as fondly recall 'Swiss rolls' of straw wrapped in black plastic. The transformation of agriculture into 'agribusiness' since the 1960s has meant that there is less and less employment for those who used to work the land: modern agriculture no longer needs, and can no longer support, a large population of rural workers.

The implications were brought home to me a few years ago when I was taken up the River Dart from Dittisham by the architect of an impressive development on the hill above that village. We were aboard the sturdy motor boat he uses for his daily commute to the office in Totnes. As we passed a picturesque hamlet beside a creek he pointed out his house, and I asked him whether the locals had accepted him yet, or indeed ever would accept an incomer.

'Ah,' he said, 'the problem doesn't really arise. I have been there twelve years, and I am now the oldest inhabitant.'

The original inhabitants are now in or around Plymouth or Exeter, where they have gone in search of employment.

Between 1950 and 1995 some 500,000 agricultural jobs disappeared and today more and more farming families are diversifying into businesses that can be run in tandem with the farms. Closest to home, literally and metaphorically, are farm shops and holiday lettings in redundant buildings or newly built cottages. Others deal in specialized foods or quality clothing by mail order, and still others offer services such as accountancy. The luckiest are those who are able to build up a parallel business which can employ their families when there is no longer enough work on the land itself.

It is at least arguable that local businesses and institutions will be able to survive, or be revived, thanks to the replacement of this disappearing agricultural population by incomers with more varied sources of livelihood, whose interest is to conserve rather than work the land.

The depopulation of rural areas is only one of many problems associated with the changing nature of Britain's countryside, and the national debate about the future of hunting, and by implication of a number of other traditional country sports, must not be allowed to obscure these. Among the organizations that give voice to the concerns of country people, the Countryside Alliance is prominent. Although it came into being because of the threat to hunting, and is best known for its campaign against its abolition, its concerns are growing very much wider. Whatever the outcome of the hunting debate, the Alliance should be a political force for the foreseeable future: the countryside needs a champion against an often urban-minded bureaucracy.

## PREPARING TO MOVE

Nowadays, although it is no longer true of some of the most sought-after areas of the South-East, there is still the very real danger that 'once you cross the county boundary, you cannot come back,' as Beatrix Potter's Pigling Bland was so memorably warned. If things go wrong, and you have made the wrong move, you may well find that the market has left you behind and you cannot afford to return to your old urban life. For this reason the possibility of letting and renting is discussed in Chapter One.

All too often people contemplating a life-changing move overlook factors that may be vital to its success. Silly season stories of townies horror-struck by sheep droppings that dirty their shiny metropolitan four-wheel drives (complete with bull bars), or who are unable to adjust to church bells and roosters, are hardly typical of most people's experience. However, they do show how sensible it is both to know your limitations and do your homework before making a firm commitment.

If so many real country men and women are leaving the countryside, it is not perhaps surprising that one reads of city people spending their bonuses, windfalls or redundancies in long-dreamed-of moves out of town, only to return in tears a couple of years later. All too often, such sparkly-eyed incomers find that reality does not immediately match up to their dreams, because they have not known the right questions to ask themselves or other people before making the vital decisions.

A move from city to country may be the most radical change of your life, whether it is to a cottage with quarter of an acre, a newly-built village house with a patch to cultivate, an old one with an established garden, a country house with paddocks, a farm or a sizeable estate. Many people would actually be happier in a market town than they would in the deep countryside, if they only paused to consider it. Battersea to the back of beyond is a large step. In any event, unless you relish the life of a hermit, you should include your social desiderata alongside the more obvious considerations: the class war may be over, as the prime minister tells us, but that does not alter the basic and quite natural truth that people feel most comfortable when they have a certain amount in common with those they meet socially.

From the physical point of view, what seems perfect at first viewing may turn out not to be so after a winter or, more serious still for many, a full school year. Friends with five children, all girls, moved out of London three or four years ago so that the family could be less cramped and the girls could have their ponies. The completion of the M40 link across Otmoor towards Birmingham had opened up south Northamptonshire and the northern corners of Oxfordshire and Buckinghamshire to serious commuting. Thus the answer appeared to be a rectory in or near the handsome, and then still comparatively cheap, village of Aynho at the southernmost tip of Northamptonshire.

A 'people carrier' was bought to supplement the car the father needed for his commute to London. The commuting was indeed fine, despite an early start. However, the other main purpose of the move was to take advantage of Oxford schooling. After a couple of terms during which she never seemed to descend from the people carrier except to fill it with petrol, the badly frayed mother had had enough. The rectory was sold (easily enough on a then rising market), and in Oxford they settled. Driving time seemed to disappear and commuting by train was generally more pleasurable than by road. Given Oxford houses and property prices, however, the ponies had to go.

So, will the area of the country that has caught your fancy meet your needs, not just so far as price and communications are concerned, but also from the social, sporting and educational points of view? It may be disastrous to plunge on a house you can afford and which looks entrancing on a summer day, in an area you feel you know well – but only from weekends or holidays.

You must also do your research if you intend to commute – underestimating the time this takes can cause much unnecessary stress – but remember that a trial journey outside the rush hour on a spring afternoon will turn out to be rather different to the reality of a January morning's expedition at 6.30 a.m. with freezing fog and a points failure outside Waterloo. The same is true of estimated and true times for school runs.

When you have done your research and found a property that appeals to you there are yet more questions to ask before you make an offer for it. How far can you depend on the vendors or the estate agent, who is, after all, *their* agent, to fill you in about the essentials of local life? And how do local and national planning regulations affect properties? You will also need to know whether the house is listed, and how that might affect restoration or alterations; and check that your survey has uncovered all the relevant circumstances of the property, such as rights of way. If farmland is included in the property you will have to decide what to do with it – unless you want to become a farmer.

If you are prone to hay fever it is worth checking on the kinds of crops that are grown in the surrounding fields. If you have little experience of gardening, you will need to decide how best a large, landscaped or well-established garden will be maintained. The local employment position is important if you are likely to need help on the land or in the house, or in running a business. The availability, or otherwise, of local services and transport is also important. There are other questions, too. Will you willingly take to mail order (and email) to supplement local shops and supermarkets? Do you have reliable friends in town who will send you anything that isn't available locally. Do you mind patronizing an out-of-town supermarket, or are you keen to preserve specialist shops and local stores?

All these are purely practical questions and some may not concern you but, before you commit yourself irrevocably to moving, it is vital to be sure that all involved are dreaming the same dreams and looking for at least a similar outcome. This is not particularly difficult, but it does require diplomacy. Just because an area has a deep resonance for one person because of family connections, happy memories of a student romance or pure self-image, it does not follow that the rest of the family will be happy. One man's castle may be one woman's dungeon; one woman's nest, one man's gin trap. The interests of a hotshot commuter – of either sex – must be sensitively melded with those of the stay-at-home teleporter, school runner, shopper, orderer of winter fuel supplies, diplomat and principal socializer with the neighbours.

Another very important point is that immediate priorities may not match future needs. There is no point in pretending that every age group has the same priorities. A couple of professionals in their thirties, recently married, no children, and previously happy in the possession of a weekend cottage, may not want or need the same things as a single person in his or her late twenties, a couple with young children, an established family with at least one commuter, or people in their fifties. Those who have actually retired have a different perspective again. Rural infrastructure and local amenities are often a secondary consideration for buyers moving out of town and establishing their first toehold in the country. However, as they grow older local facilities become ever more important.

# SETTLING IN

A bee that constantly buzzes in my bonnet is that people enjoy their lives and surroundings much more if they are aware of at least a little history. If you are an incomer to an area, history will not only be a useful aid in understanding your new neighbours, but will also allow you to get the feel of a landscape. On occasions it can even be an aid to successful property buying. As I suggest in Chapter Seven, a knowledge of the Dissolution of the Monasteries could be useful if you are in search of a well-tempered garden. This is a theory of my own that has yet to be tested widely – but you will have read it here first.

History is also invaluable in teaching us about the diversity of the people who live in the countryside. London, along with New York, is recognized as one of the world's greatest international cities, but very few of the populations of English and Welsh counties are homogenous communities of individuals with closely similar genes. If ever you think that you are being made to feel an interloper, rather than just an incomer, remember that in this country almost everybody came from somewhere else; it is just a question of how recently.

The possibility of friction between inhabitants and incomers exists in any society. It may as easily occur after a move from one city street to the next as in a village. Nor is it a particularly British phenomenon. On a visit to Colorado a couple of years ago I read the following in the *Denver Post*: 'Oregon town feud mirrors changes across the West – newcomers' actions irk oldtimers'. This story, characterized by one of those involved as 'Old West vs New West, drip coffee vs espresso, Bud vs microbrew, RV parks vs bed and breakfasts, and worms vs. fly fishing', has its counterparts in many a British village. You may recall the millionaire motor dealer and his wife who complained that sheep had made a road adjoining their land too muddy.

Tales such as these might be enough to put anyone off venturing beyond the city limits. The experiences of the brave souls who are not put off are normally quite different. A most encouraging instance comes from the Lincoln office of the estate agents FDPSavills.

They had a good deal of interest in Manor Farm, not an untypical property for the area, and in line with the trend for many farm sales nowadays they offered it in two lots. Lot 1 was the main five-bedroom, four-reception-room house with outbuildings including a coach house and a stone-built barn and wash house, along with 12 acres of paddock. This went to Malcolm and Bernadette Hornby, who had moved from Banbury. Lot 2 was the remaining 131 acres of arable land and was bought by a local farmer.

The Hornbys bought the house after doing their homework thoroughly, as would be expected of a management consultant who is the author of an excellent book on getting the best out of life (see Directory, page 226).

'Our move was completely based on quality of life,' Mr Hornby wrote afterwards. 'The city of Lincoln is beautiful with excellent facilities, some unexpected, such as the opportunity to sail our boat from its moorings at Brayford Pool, right in the heart of the city. The county's towns and villages have a lovely, unspoilt feel about them, but most importantly, the people of Lincolnshire are amongst the most friendly, helpful and genuinely welcoming people I have ever met. We really feel at home here.

'Bernadette and I sat down with a blank piece of paper and used the techniques I advocated in my book to map out the rest of our lives. Now here we are in Lincolnshire.

'People say "but isn't Lincolnshire a bit off the beaten track?" but they shouldn't live in the past. The recently completed dualling of the A1, the excellent rail link from Grantham, and the pending dualling of the A46 are all shrinking the county. But for me the most significant factor is the use of electronic communications. I can sit in my study and watch pheasants and hedgehogs running past my window, while sending a proposal through the Internet to my clients anywhere in the country.

'As to price – I'm sure our friends must think we've won the lottery. Property prices in Lincolnshire are unbelievably good value compared to down south. I'm sure they are bound to rise, as more people like us catch on.'

They didn't actually need the paddock that went with the house, but saw it as a good long-term investment that would provide future owners with a ready-made pony paddock. In the meantime they have rented it to a neighbouring farmer, perhaps at slightly below the going rate, but that made more sense than contract farming.

This book is intended if not to answer, then at least to offer advice on, some of the questions a move to the country raises, and to suggest patterns of thinking, direct and lateral, which may help to circumvent difficulties commonly met by people who settle there. The particular problems of gardens, parcels of farmland – those intending to farm seriously must be presumed to know what they are about – planning, holiday homes and weekend cottages will be considered. The section surveying the different counties and areas of England and Wales may perhaps also ease the way for experienced country people who are moving from one region to another. Perhaps, too, it will give the many foreigners who settle here for longer or shorter periods, some idea of the people among whom they find themselves. The estate agent's witticism that the three most important things in property buying are location, location and location, may have become a cliché, but it is still very true.

# CHAPTER ONE

# ACQUIRING
# A PROPERTY:
# THE FIRST STEPS

Deciding whether to live in a village or in an isolated country property could be vital to your future happiness. The sheer diversity of choice – of area, kind of house and even type of society – is one of the main themes of this book. On a summer's day the North Yorkshire moors can be very close to heaven. But no one, surely, would decide to live there without even sampling a winter. That may seem obvious enough, but people do sometimes make such life-determining decisions without considering their social needs and preferences, which can be quite as important to their happiness as climatic conditions.

Even neighbouring counties can differ socially as well as physically. For instance, Cumbria has many traditional 'gentry' country properties and village and country-town houses, which means that visiting, dining, dancing, children's parties and general socializing are possible without too much driving. In Northumberland, on the other hand, such a social life would be more difficult as there are far fewer 'gentry' properties – most are either castles or working farms, especially in the north of the county. Local information of this sort is often the key to success-ful settlement.

In 1989 *Country Life* and Knight Frank & Rutley (as they still were) jointly published a guide called *Buying a Country House* (see Directory, page 226). It included many ideas and much information that I have incorporated in updated form in this book, although my scope is very much wider. One of the introductory paragraphs was so full of good sense that it should be compulsory reading for every would-be house buyer, in town or country, to learn it by heart before looking at a list or visiting an agent. I quote it here in full:

'People usually talk for years about moving house, then embark upon it in a rush. They discuss the subject endlessly, but may do little research. Frequently their first ideas of what they will find are quite over-optimistic. Unless you are very rich or very lucky, the house you buy will be a compromise. So don't expect perfection: you are unlikely to find it. Moreover, it can be a distrac-tion: while you are searching for perfection you may well miss the house that *is* right for you, but since you saw it at the beginning of your quest you dismissed it for the most insignificant of reasons.'

## STATISTICS

One of the few generalizations worth noting when house-hunting is that generalizations about prices are worthless. Building soci-eties are particularly fond of them, and all too frequently property journalists in need of copy waste whole pages on such topics as: 'Prices in what Nationwide describes as the "outer South-East", which includes the Chilterns, south Buckinghamshire and parts of Essex and the Home Counties, have increased by only 45 per cent,' and: 'the average house now costs £79,029 in the outer South-East, up from £54,455 in 1993'. When even a mews in London's Holland Park can have a right and a wrong end, how can a percentage rise or fall over an area of several thousand square miles have any practical meaning? Similarly, the 'average house' is as commonly met with as the family with 2.2 children.

# RENTING

If you have never lived in the country before, or at least not in your adult lifetime, this is perhaps the point at which you should consider whether you should be buying at all. This is not an attempt to put you off entirely. Rather, it is a reminder that not all available property in the country is for sale, and that a trial period in a rented house will help you to decide whether you really do like a particular area, or indeed country living. Renting also makes good sense if you want a second home, or believe that it is best for your children to be brought up away from the smoke but suspect that you will want to return there once they have flown the nest.

William Gething, of the buying agents Property Vision, has rented two properties in Dorset over the last fourteen years or so. The first was a second home, the second is intended to be permanent. Over that time he has noted a phenomenal rise in demand for country rentals, certainly in Dorset but also elsewhere. To some extent this must reflect improving communications and the fact that people are prepared to travel greater distances in search of a saner way of life.

The ideal situation is one in which you let your urban property at the same time as you rent in the country. To use London and Dorset as examples once again, at present a good London property should yield around 6 per cent gross of its market value. Even after paying 40 per cent income/capital gains tax and standard management fees (15 per cent plus VAT) this will cover the 3 per cent rental you could expect to pay in Dorset. This enables you to keep your equity and either sell if the market rises or return to London should you wish to do so.

Obviously, these figures can change either upwards or down; the 6 per cent has been fairly static over the last year or so, while the 3 per cent is gradually rising. However, the town and country rental markets are significantly different and the general ratio is not likely to alter, except in specific areas. In cities, and London especially, rentals are dominated by international corporations and other large companies that can set off what they pay against profits. In the country, tenants are generally mere British mortals who pay in real post-tax pounds. If a property is their 'permanent' home they are likely to work locally, in which case their salaries may be less than those of urban executives, while tenants for whom it is a second home are likely to run their lives on a budget. For these reasons country rentals tend to remain relatively low.

Leaving aside people who let as a business, and others who subdivide a house that is too large for them, there are essentially two reasons for country owners to let property. One is that they are being posted abroad and need to find running costs, house sitters and perhaps income for between one and three years. Another is when properties on large estates are not currently needed by estate workers or the owner's family. These are likely to be on longer leases and there are sometimes deals to be done. For instance, you may undertake to do up or redecorate the house in lieu of rent. Most houses, though, are let empty and on a repairing basis. Sometimes paying for improvements that will ultimately benefit someone else can be irksome, but most good tenants will be happy to invest time and a certain amount of money in keeping up a decent garden. They would be unlikely to have taken on the house otherwise. Even if it is not quite pride of ownership there is a kind of pride in knowing that what you have planted and left behind will flourish for years or generations. Naturally a good short-term tenant will not alienate a valued gardener or any other help.

Country tenants must resign themselves to the wearisome fact, however, that they cannot always expect the immediate attention from agents when things go wrong that they might be accorded in a city let. If the plumber is busy, they just have to wait on his pleasure. As a consolation, remember that the best craftsman is the one who is most booked up.

# BUYING

*Buying a Country House* continued with another point that it is essential for any buyer to understand at the outset: the agent who is selling the house is being paid by the owner to act on his behalf and get him the best price, not by you to get you the best deal. Since the Property Misdescriptions Act came into force in 1991 it is no longer safe for an agent to fill his brochures with unprovable theories and speculative claims about a property's history, architecture and structural state. However, it is not necessarily part of his business to point out drawbacks to potential purchasers at an early stage, or indeed at any stage, unless he is asked about them.

Some years ago I had to write a short note in *Country Life* about a former church in Yorkshire which had been converted to a house and was then on the market, prettily pictured in its sale brochure. I had not actually visited it but had the lucky thought that, since it would not then have been redundant, it would probably be mentioned in my 1960s copy of John Betjeman's *English Parish Churches*. It was: 'The lack of self-consciousness of builders working in an alive vernacular and its happy results are thrown into sharp relief by the contrast between this church and the adjoining brutal new pumping station.' A call to the agents established that the pumping station, although no longer so new, was still just as brutal.

Of course, that would have been evident to anyone who visited the property, but the agents were hoping that the charm and character of the building itself, together with a realistic price, would offset the problem. As I recall, they were right.

Common sense tells us not to insist on perfection. Almost everyone who has ever picked up a copy of *Country Life*, in the dentist's waiting room or anywhere else, has had fantasies about a beautiful Georgian house nestling in a few acres of parkland on the edge of a village, with nothing to be heard but skylarks and the buzzing of bees. But even Highgrove has road noise, and Blenheim has a footpath. You must never be afraid to compromise, as long as your core requirements are met. It often helps to draw up a list of all the features you are looking for, and mark them from one to ten in order of importance. This will give you an idea of the areas where you might be happy to compromise.

However commonsensical you are, you just may get carried away and decide you simply must have a property that is quite the opposite to what you had intended. If it is an unusual feature that has hooked you, it would be wise to seek specialist advice before you plunge irrevocably and make an offer. This may confirm your passion, or it may save you a considerable sum.

A surveyor tells me that the best £100 he ever spent was early in his career when he was called in to look at his first thatched roof. Rather than pretend he knew what he was looking at and for, he contacted a thatcher who agreed to accompany him. What he learned as a result has stood him in good stead throughout his subsequent career.

In the same way, local knowledge, whether obtained from neighbours, an agent on the spot or a surveyor, can be invaluable. Such a person may be able to tell you about drawbacks – or advantages – unknown to a national agent. Building materials are a prime example. For instance, in the nineteenth century an artificial building stone, masdic block, was developed around Mousehole in Cornwall. Unfortunately, while it might have been perfect for use inland it was not suited to the salt winds of the Cornish coast and, where it has survived, it causes problems for house-owners. Similarly, the local stone that was used for many prominent buildings in the Leeds area of Yorkshire was too soft to withstand attacks by acid pollution during the industrial era, and seems to suffer again when subjected to cleaning.

Of course some drawbacks may not be at all obvious even after you have spoken to someone with local knowledge, had a careful look around and taken the precaution of studying a detailed map (see Directory, page 225). I once bought a London house that was thoroughly shaken by passing buses except, by a quirk of the timetable, during the late afternoon or early evening – the periods when I had most often been able to view it. It was a long time before I got any sleep there. In the country, combine harvesters and farm traffic, rather than the all too few rural buses, are more likely to disturb you. Remember that weekend viewing, which is often the only practicable option for busy people, may not disclose everything you should perhaps know. The following checklist may help.

## CHECKLIST FOR BUYERS

ADJOINING LAND: It could sometimes make all the difference to a property if you were able to buy a next-door field or neighbouring parcel of land. If you suspect that this would ensure your privacy, enable you to carry out gardening schemes, keep animals or protect you from developers, see if it is possible to buy it. The price might go up at a later stage when it becomes evident that you simply must have the land.

BOUNDARIES: Check your boundaries and the ownership of any boundary hedges, walls or fences. It is as well to know from the outset who is responsible for the maintenance of what, especially if your property borders on several others. Quarrels about boundaries can bedevil relationships with neighbours – even without *leylandii*. Agents are sometimes a little vague about what exactly you are buying. My mother-in-law discovered too late that she actually owned the ideal corner in which to put her oil tank. It is obviously important to respect the traditions of an area, so you may also need to find out whether you will have to employ specialist hedgers, drystone wallers or fencers for the boundaries that you have to maintain. Stream and river boundaries should also be checked as they may involve riparian and fishing rights.

CESSPITS: Find out if there is one, where it is and whether it is efficient. Also check if there have ever been problems with neighbouring cesspits overflowing or seeping on to your land.

DISTANCES: How far is it to the shops, supermarket and post office; the doctor and hospital? This information is crucial. Many areas of the country lack these basic facilities and with local buses rare or even non-existent, and the nearest railway station frequently miles away, a car is often the only option. Driving in the country is less stressful than in towns, and distances seem to diminish, but before deciding on a property it is sensible to decide just how far you are prepared to go in search of a stamp or a pint of milk.

ENVIRONMENT: Check whether there are any agri-businesses in the vicinity of the property – and what they are. While the consequences of living downwind from a sugar-beet refinery will only be evident in the winter months, a silage pit or a battery hen house could be a more permanent nuisance.

It may save sufferers from migraine or hay fever future discomfort if they inform themselves about regular crops in nearby fields, and what pesticides and fertilizers are in frequent use. A very useful web site for anyone seriously worried about pollutants in the air is one organized by Friends of the Earth to monitor factory emissions (see Directory, page 226). Similar sites cover traffic pollution.

FLOODING: A stream or river is often the feature that attracts a buyer to a particular house but, however enthusiastic you are about water gardening, fishing or simply messing about in boats, you would be wise to enquire if it is prone to flooding. This is particularly important if you are looking for a weekend home as you won't be around to deal with any floods that occur during the week. Some unexpected places do flood, but only once every fifty years or so. You should take a view on this, and on whether insurance is worthwhile. If you are in an area such as the Severn Valley check for flooding anyway, even if you are not actually close to the river. Flooding apart, if you have young children you may have to take precautions if a stream or river runs through the property.

GARAGES AND OUTHOUSES: Be sure there is adequate garaging. In town a garage can be seen as an optional extra, but in the country it is much more necessary: large cities are warmer than much of the countryside – London temperatures are on average 2°C higher than those in Suffolk, for instance – and heavy snowfalls and freezing weather are less likely to immobilize cars parked outside town houses. You may also need somewhere secure for storing gardening equipment, especially if you run to a minitractor, and for bicycles, mopeds or quad bikes.

NEIGHBOURS: Neighbours may not seem to be a problem in the country but if they are relatively close by they should be checked if at all possible. If a village property is next door to a large family house with a swimming pool, you must realize that your sunbathing or gardening afternoons could be less peaceful than you might wish. This would only be a problem during the warmer months, but a nearby pub could be a year-round nuisance if customers have to walk, park or drive along a lane beside your house.

A cautionary tale regarding the importance of neighbours, boundaries and, indeed, land, comes from a surveyor who was asked to look at a property in Essex on behalf of a potential purchaser. It was an interesting old house, and it came with seven or eight acres, including two paddocks. This pleased the hopeful purchaser, since he had pony-aged children and intended to indulge them (see Chapter Nine). However, a neighbour made him what appeared to be the very handsome offer of £40,000 for the larger paddock should he succeed in acquiring the property. It would more than cover fees and moving costs.

The surveyor pointed out that the smaller paddock would not support a couple of ponies and perhaps a donkey. Even if hay were bought in, the plot would be a mudbath after autumn and spring. He also found out that the larger paddock adjoined perhaps the most prestigious golf course in the area, and that owners of bordering properties enjoyed automatic membership rights. This may well have been the real reason behind the neighbour's pre-emptive offer.

The surveyor advised the potential purchaser to keep the paddock, at least until he had thought things through, as the right must add to the resale value of the property. Also, before the family actually acquired any ponies they could offer to rent the grazing to the neighbour – and continue to do so later if the paddocks would bear it.

The lesson is very clear: accept no kindly offers, even if they will apparently ease your path in buying a property, until you know exactly what is involved. Established neighbours know much better than you what its various features are worth to them. Unneighbourly feelings will persist for some time if you discover that you have been asset-stripped.

NOISE AND NUISANCES: Although most people move to the country in search of peace and quiet, it is worth making sure this is what you will get. Check whether the property is near a farm – its traffic can be a nuisance. And if the property is anywhere near an airport make sure your surveyor checks local flight paths. It is much easier to get used to the hum of a major road than to roaring jumbo jets – and flight paths are inescapable. A recent court case in which a buyer was awarded damages of £10,750 against a surveyor who failed to do this underscores the need for thoroughness. The buyer wanted to be sure that his croquet, swimming and pre-dinner drinks would not be disturbed by aircraft noise – understandably, since the property was only 15 miles (24 kilometres) from Gatwick Airport. Somehow the surveyor overlooked the fact that the house was close to a navigation beacon, and that the area was in fact badly affected by circling aircraft, particularly at weekends. He admitted that he had indeed discussed the subject with the buyer but claimed, unsuccessfully, that he had not had precise and particular instructions.

Some problems are strictly seasonal. The noise from a motorbike scramble course or four-wheel-car racing is likely to be much more intrusive in summer than in winter and, similarly, aircraft noise from a flying club in the vicinity may only become a nuisance at certain times of day, month or year, or when the wind is in a particular direction. Obviously, any summer viewer should check whether thick foliage is lessening traffic noise that will increase in winter (as well as disguising anything unsightly).

PLANNED DEVELOPMENTS: It is vital to find out if there is any likelihood of building developments on neighbouring land, as well as proposed road and other transport improvements that might impinge on the property or area. Ask about these when you discuss an appointment to view with the agent, who should allude at this point to any problems he knows of so as not to waste both your time and the vendor's. In addition, make sure that your agent or solicitor pesters the council about any as yet unannounced intentions, and government plans, during the searches. Local authorities can be cagey, as can the Ministry of Transport. Given the current enthusiasm for new housing, this kind of investigation will become an increasingly important. Planning blight can sometimes work to the advantage of a purchaser, provided he gets first knowledge that it is likely to be lifted.

RIGHTS OF WAY AND INFORMAL ARRANGEMENTS: Find out whether anyone has legal rights or customary usage of the property. Are there any public footpaths or rights of way? Do scouts or guides have the use of a hut? Does the local hunt meet nearby, or does a fishing club have an agreement to use your river bank? Are any fairs set up close to the house? Your buying agent or solicitor should be able to reassure you on such points, but it would be wise also to consult the vendors and neighbours.

WEATHER: Find out if there are frost pockets, or places where snow banks up, especially if the property is surrounded by narrow lanes – you may need to add the price of a four-wheel drive to the cost of moving. Similarly, are there any climatic conditions such as prevailing winds that could affect planting plans in the garden?

# NEW WAYS OF BUYING

The traditional routine of weekend after weekend spent in a car filled with estate agents' details, scouring your chosen area, is no longer the only practical way to secure the country property you want. Today, it is also possible to use the technology of the Internet or the more personal services of a buying agent, in conjunction with traditional estate agents, to find the house you want.

THE INTERNET: The recent rapid growth in the use of the Internet to find properties should make it easier to discover some of the necessary information at earlier stages. One of the largest umbrella sites at present is Internet Property Finder (see Directory, page 226). IPF and its fellows allow people to make preliminary enquiries without huge expenditure of time and petrol, obviously a considerable advantage for anyone who plans to move a long way from their present home.

IPF quotes the example of a couple who wanted to move from London to countryside within reach of Preston, Lancashire. Weekends spent driving about the target area helped to familiarize them with the opportunities, and they took down estate agents' names from the boards in villages. However, they could not hope to track down every agent, and all too often even those they did find failed to send lists or details. The web allowed them to contact agents in advance and arrange viewings so that they were able to spend the weekends much more profitably. Their only complaint was that some agents failed to update their sites often enough, but this will soon change as the new marketing tool is seen to work.

Other important points of call for Net users are listed in the Directory (page 226) and include *Country Life*'s own award-winning site, which will put you well ahead of the game.

BUYING AGENTS: For most people, even the very rich, a property purchase is likely to be one of the biggest outlays of their lives. Yet only a tiny proportion of house-buyers seek the services of an expert. It is not that such expertise cannot be obtained, nor that it is outrageously expensive. Not only do several leading estate agents, including Knight Frank, Savills and Bidwells, have departments with both house-finders and skilled negotiators, but there are a number of experienced and reputable firms that specialize in buying properties on behalf of clients.

Buying agents have been around since the early 1980s. It is their business to be aware of all relevant developments that may affect the character of an area, and to acquaint themselves thoroughly with the needs, circumstances and tastes of a client. Furthermore, it is part of their expertise to ferret out any reasons for a sale which it may be advantageous for the buyer to know. Death? Divorce? Criminal proceedings, business problems or Lloyds?

The late cartoonist and comedian Willie Rushton once bought a splendid Thames-side property (in Cookham Dean) for well below the market value because, as it emerged later, the vendor's problems with the Mafia necessitated a fast cash sale. Had a buying agent been available in those days, the price might have been yet lower. Mrs Rushton would also have been spared an uncomfortable half hour some weeks after moving in, when a very large visitor took her for the wife of the previous owner.

Buying agents charge between 1 per cent or 2 per cent of the purchase price and to be worthwhile they should save a client more than this through their searching and negotiating skills. A further advantage is that when the deal is concluded many agents are happy to provide management and other services to get, and keep, the property running.

Neither the Internet nor buying agents mean that estate agents are a thing of the past. Despite the wide-boy image some of them have acquired, they are a very necessary oil in facilitating property transactions and will continue to be so. Nevertheless, although they are not under threat from the Internet to the extent that, say, travel agents are, the Net will take over some of their traditional functions and they are having to be quick on their feet. A few years ago, a number of middle-sized provincial agents realized that they needed to have a London shop window, where their brochures could be seen and studied, if they were to compete with national and international firms with large advertising budgets. This was the origin of The London Office (see Directory, page 226), which is a good first stop in any search for a property, especially if you want to compare what is available in different areas. It also gives the smaller firms a weighty joint presence on the Net.

## ETIQUETTE FOR VIEWERS

The following points apply as much to viewing in town as in the country, but the importance of establishing good relations with sellers cannot be over-emphasized.

◆ Don't waste a vendor's (or an agent's) time. It is sometimes excusable, and indeed advisable, to view places that are unlikely to be right for you, to get a feel for what is possible in an area, but make sure that the agent understands what you are about.

◆ Seeing a few bad houses will help you to recognize a good one. And remember that partners really must visit properties together.

◆ Don't view houses you have no interest in buying just because you've always wanted to look inside. That is the privilege of the property journalist.

◆ Do turn up for appointments – and try not to be late.

◆ Don't wreck Sunday lunch.

◆ Never talk about alterations and improvements as if the vendors were not there. They may decide not to sell. To you, at any rate.

◆ Never, ever, criticize a kitchen, however poky or primitive it seems. I did this once, mildly, in print. It was poky, and thirty-five years overdue for redecoration and re-equipping – but goodness, what a fuss.

◆ Make sure you know how you are going to raise the money in case you want something and have to move quickly. The estate agent will quite rightly advise his client to look further if you are unable to perform. Some local agents will not bother even to register enquirers from town who are only 'thinking about' a move.

◆ Buyers often think their budget will go further if they buy a ruin and restore it. This can be true (see Chapter Four). However, in the property world one ruin has been known to lead to another – your own.

## THE BEST OF ALL POSSIBLE SALES

The keys to a trouble-free transaction are speed and diligence on the part of buyer, seller and agent. Many problems can be avoided if both sides are fully prepared to buy and sell. Sometimes seemingly enthusiastic buyers have not begun to sell their own house, or are dependent on an untrustworthy chain for their financing. Sometimes an eager would-be purchaser finds that the seller has none of the documentation ready, or that the deeds are still locked in the bank, and a few weeks may pass before even a draft contract is sent out. If all finances and documentation are ready, both sides have the opportunity to assess each other's seriousness.

An example of the ideal transaction was the sale of a farmhouse near Farnham in Hampshire. The brochures went out on a Wednesday, and the property starred on the first page of *Country Life* the following day. The purchaser viewed that Friday afternoon and made an offer on the Saturday, which was accepted on the Monday. The two sides and their solicitors met face to face on the Wednesday and contracts were exchanged that afternoon. Had nothing been prepared in advance, this simply would not have been possible.

Of course, buying any house, but especially a house in the country, is far from a doddle. At least in a London street you are likely to find several comparable, or even exactly identical, properties for comparison. Some will be in better condition than others, and some may have an additional bedroom or a smaller garden. But valuation is relatively straightforward and, if you fail to get No. 23, No. 24 may come on to the market soon after. By contrast, country properties tend to be one-offs. In the upper reaches of the market it happens quite often that only half a dozen comparable houses are sold in any one county and any one year. And these may be comparable only in the sense that they are 'good' houses, for how do you compare a sixteenth-century manor house at the end of a long drive with a Georgian rectory on the edge of a village?

The outcome is that there is rarely an asking price, especially if the market is volatile. Every estate agent has his own style of selling. Some ask for a very high sum and negotiate towards it. Others pitch a guide price that is round about the figure at which they expect the property to sell. Still others quote a price 'in excess of' in an attempt to generate competitive bidding; buyers who misunderstand this may offer the quoted figure thinking it to be the asking price, and find themselves left behind in the slip-stream. Many purchasers find the competitive element disturbing, but it is part and parcel of the reality of buying a country property and the quicker you accept this, the more likely you are to succeed.

On the other hand, unless speed really is of the essence, it is best not to allow yourself to be rushed. You can be certain that as soon as you have made the offer the agent's telephone lines will be red-hot as he drums up competition. Try to pay cash if you can. In the country, as in town, everyone loves a cash buyer, so organize your finances accordingly. Remember that any bid that is subject to the sale of another house puts you right at the bottom of the pile.

If you pitch your initial offer too low you could irritate the vendor and won't be the favoured bidder if a choice has to be made. When all things are equal on price, the personal relationship is the key. So it may facilitate a deal if you are willing to try to fit in with the vendor's ideas about timescales and moving arrangements.

Good manners and common sense are the most important characteristics of a successful buyer. It is good manners, as well as good sense, to remember that selling a property in the country is every bit as stressful as buying one; sellers have both financial and emotional capital tied up in the house. Even if you believe you are stealing it from them, you should never let them feel it. Quite possibly one of the three Ds – Death, Debt or Divorce – has triggered the sale and, if so, you will have to allow for that emotional baggage. Tact and understanding go a long way, and the old adage of leaving something in the deal for the other person is as true as it ever was.

It can be counter-productive to push vendors too far. Once you have bought your property you will inherit more than just bricks and mortar from the previous owners, and you do not want them poisoning the well either metaphorically or literally. They will provide local people with their first information about

# Buying and Selling

## MARKETING

Your house is worth £450,000 and your estate agent will urge you to advertise your house. Being a good agent, he will advise a page in Country Life:

£3,500 + VAT = £3,575

He will also prepare your imposing brochure:

£1,500 + VAT = £1,762.50

Success! You have sold your house and got your price – but you keep on spending.

## Commission

Your agent will now claim his percentage of £450,000, say 2 per cent:

£9,000

Persuade him to wait until after the sale is completed before receiving payment – you should certainly not hand over the fee until you are assured that everything has gone according to plan and that you, or rather your solicitor – fees coming up – has the cheque. Thus you are at least deferring the VAT, but in due course:

£9,000 + VAT = £10,575

## Legal fees

If your solicitor is reasonable, and you must insist that he is, he will agree to defer his fees on the sale until after the purchase of your new property. But do not forget that you owe him, say:

£1,800 + VAT = £2,115

## BUYING

You decide to use a buying agent. Watch out for the fees in relation to the actual value of the service you receive, or may not receive (remember, he should save you more than the commission he will charge). Read the fine print of any contract with the agent with a magnifying glass, and preferably ask your solicitor to do the same (for an increased fee). If you are careless, or happen on a rogue agent, you could end up paying commission for a house that you found for yourself. In any event the agent's fee might be 1.5 per cent or more. You agree on a property priced at a modest £300,000, so a finder's fee is £4,500:

£4,500 + VAT = £5,287.50

A handsome £150,000 profit, or very nearly, you tell yourself. But...

## Surveyor's fees
Perhaps:

£1,200 + VAT = £1,410

## Duty
Stamp duty is 2.5 per cent – and even the Treasury would blush to charge VAT on that. Current rates are: up to £60,000, none; to £250,000, 1 per cent; to £500,000, 2.5 per cent; above £500,00, 3.5 per cent. So:

£11,250

## Moving costs
For a reasonable household and no frills:

£1,800 + VAT         = £2,115

## More legal fees
Say another £1,300 + the iniquitous but inevitable VAT:

£1,527.50

## GRAND TOTAL:
£39,617.50

So your 'profit' on selling and buying, which looked like £150,000, is actually £110,382.50 after your solicitor has paid himself and your other creditors.

you – and neighbours are more important to your well-being in the country than they are in the comparative anonymity of a town or city.

## THE HIDDEN COSTS

Even if you have conducted the ideal transaction there is, inevitably, more expense to come. Most house-buyers are also sellers, whether the property they are selling is in a town or the country. When you are doing your initial back-of-the-envelope calculations of what you can afford it is possible to overlook some of the expenses that crop up along the way, so I give an example of overall costs, although they obviously also apply to transactions in cities. The figures are based on selling a house worth £450,000 but, with the exception of stamp duty, the ratios stay more or less the same regardless of the price of the property.

Remember that it is as well to look at a lot of small print, and a lot of small numbers, when you are doing your final calculations. Hidden costs can add up to as much as 10 per cent of the outlay when you are buying a new property.

There could be ways of shaving some of the costs I've listed. Given a hot property market in which an estate agent need only spend money on advising clients that there is a queue of potential buyers, and on a pocket calculator to work out his – and your – percentages, it *might* not be necessary to advertise, or to spend so much – if anything – on a brochure. Your agent *might* even be amenable to some reduction of his percentage. You might well decide to forego the buying agent as being a luxury – but remember that legwork costs time and petrol. With the pressure of earning a living, many people tend to leave it to the professionals and pay accordingly.

Solicitors and surveyors are obviously essential, and are usually good value. Opinions may be divided on the comparative values of the various other services, but there can be no two opinions on the Chancellor's various 17.5 per cents and the stamp duty – he gets his slice of practically everything.

# CHAPTER TWO

# WEEKEND, HOLIDAY AND RETIREMENT HOMES

No one has calculated the figures exactly, but it is esti-mated that about 250,000 properties in Britain are second homes. From the Chilterns to the West Country, whole swathes of countryside have been opened to weekend-cottage owners from London. The M40 extension has made Northamptonshire possible from both London and Birmingham, and Wales has seen a renewed movement from Birmingham, Liverpool and Manchester. In the north Scots from Glasgow and Edinburgh are making their weekend presence felt in Cumbria and, particularly, Northumberland. North Norfolk is more the preserve of families in need of summer holiday access to the sea but Suffolk, long a poor cousin, attracts more and more weekend commuters, especially since money still goes a good deal further in much of East Anglia than in the true Home Counties.

There are a variety of reasons for this weekly exodus from the cities and, before looking at any areas, let alone properties, you need to know precisely what you want from a second home. You should also have a good idea of how often you will actually use it – and whether you can afford two lots of heating bills, telephone rentals and so on.

For some people a priority is the need for a lung to carry them through city life during the week, or to provide their children with one. If children are the reason, it may be sensible to choose somewhere they, and you, already have friends. Some people may want to be in reach of elderly parents, but not next door to them or in their pockets. Others see a weekend cottage as a preparatory stage for a more complete move later. There are many people who want to enjoy a particular country pursuit, such as sailing, golf, hang-gliding, walking or riding, and its availability may possibly dictate their choice of area. Still others buy properties as investments, in some cases to provide themselves with a future retirement home. And, of course, there are people who are actually retiring. All these groups are likely to require rather different things of their ideal property.

Undoubtedly, for most people the most important consideration when choosing a weekend home is the journey time from town. At present the consensus among estate agents is that one and a half hours – by rail or car – is generally acceptable, and that only the most hardy people, or those whose weekends revolve around pastimes in particular places, will be happy with longer journeys. This is naturally only a rule of thumb since, if you are driving, the distance you can cover in one and a half hours depends on your route from the city – and it obviously helps if you are not constrained to travel on Friday and Sunday evenings. Another factor that is important for many people, and may govern the amount of use they actually make of a property, is whether pets will travel happily.

Even if you intend to drive to your weekend home, it is as well to choose somewhere within reach of a good rail service for school holidays and other times when the whole family may not be returning at the same time. In that case you could look at properties a little further away from stations than would suit regular daily commuters, as their prices should be lower.

Once you have decided on the location of your weekend home there will be many other decisions to make. Do you want a house where you can easily have friends to stay? Will you able to heat it up quickly? How will you maintain the garden if you are not there during the week? Don't put off considerations of such points until after you have bought, because they will largely determine the use and pleasure that you get from the home.

# SECURITY

It is natural that weekenders and owners of holiday homes should be concerned about security when their properties are left empty and this, together with easy access to the local shop (if any) and pub (if any) for drinks and Sunday lunches, means that the most popular and expensive properties for second homes are in or on the edges of villages.

For the record, in 1996 the estate agents John D.Wood reported that in Oxfordshire 86.5 per cent of their clients wanted houses on the edges of villages, and that this was increasing prices by around 10 per cent. A similar story was repeated by Mullucks Wells, an agent operating in the counties around Saffron Walden. However, if a village becomes too popular with weekenders and holiday visitors, there will be fewer full-time neighbours to keep an eye on things. It is important to enquire about this before making an investment as friendly neighbours are the best security and, ideally, will check your property regularly.

It would also be wise to seek advice from the local crime prevention police officer. Lighting and curtain timers, window locks and perhaps outside security lights triggered by movement are all useful, but the outside lights should be arranged so that they do not go off for every passing cat and fox, or the neighbours may take less notice of them. A middle-aged – but not decrepit – car parked in the drive provides additional security. If it is taxed it will be also useful when you are there. It is obviously sensible to telephone neighbours in advance if you lend your cottage to friends, so that the police are not summoned to deal with intruders.

However perfect it may be in every other respect, a really isolated cottage with no neighbours within sight or sound is not a good buy for weekenders if security is a concern for them. Others may consider isolation to be the perfect antidote to weekly existence in the city, but they will need bars and bolts. If you do settle on a property outside the village but in a farming district, and near to a road, observant neighbours can be supplemented by the local FarmWatch (see Chapter Five), especially if you are willing to lend a hand when in residence.

## LOCAL FEELINGS

Empty second homes may not just be security problems for their owners; in particularly popular areas they may also be a cause of understandable, and sometimes quite considerable, resentment among the established inhabitants. There are a wealth of reaons why weekenders might be resented, but one of the main ones is that young people are perceived as no longer being able to afford homes in the places where they were born and brought up.

The most extreme manifestation of opposition to second homes was the rash of nationalist arson attacks on English-owned cottages in north and mid-Wales during the 1970s. This was linked to wider political issues such as language and water, and is happily long past. More recently, however, problems for young local buyers have arisen in other areas of the country because of the high prices willingly paid by outsiders. An example is the Scilly Isles, where housing is in any case limited. In the summer of 1999 property values had outstripped those in Cornwall, the nearest mainland county, and were approaching levels seen in near-central London.

The situation in holiday areas is likely to be more difficult than elsewhere in this regard, since flats and cottages run as holiday-letting businesses are withdrawn from the pool of available homes. Furthermore, such areas tend to attract retired settlers who are able to pay higher prices. However, planning authorities around the country are increasingly aware of the problem, and in some cases planning permission has been granted more readily for developments of new 'executive' houses when they include lower-priced housing for local people.

In time, of course, many second homes will become first ones, and their owners will themselves become locals. Weekenders who intend to settle in an area at a later date often find it best to work themselves in by taking part in fêtes, fairs and local events, showing at least an interest in the church and using nearby shops and pubs. It all helps to demonstrate a commitment and can easily be done without acquiring a reputation for being pushy. More than lip service is needed to preserve local facilities and, after all, any shopkeeper might resent the sight of metropolitan supplies for a whole weekend being unloaded from pristine four-wheel drives and estates on a Friday evening.

A slow but steady infiltration is best and, as ever, is often most easily accomplished by people with children. Even if you decide to change your property at a later stage, if you wish to remain in the area you will remember that the early impressions you make will naturally matter.

# LETTING

Many people who buy a country property while they are comfortably living elsewhere, either as a holiday home or a place to retire to in a few years, will naturally think of letting it out to earn its keep in the meantime. If this is your intention, you should consider your purchase from the points of view of present and future needs. The rent should provide a little income as well as covering costs, but it may turn out that a property that was a sound letting investment during your working years is not the place you want to retire to.

If you are currently working, the present needs of your potential tenants may not coincide with those of your leisured self later on. Tenants may need to be close to a station, schools or entertainments, which may not matter to you when you retire. Perhaps more importantly, a family of tenants might want a sizeable garden, while your future preference could be for something small enough to make no great physical demands. Similarly, stairs may not worry them, but could become tiresome for you. It could be sensible to buy twice: first for the best income, and second for what is best for you.

Before deciding to buy to let, it is as well to take the advice of the lettings specialist at the local estate agent. They should know what is likely to attract tenants and will also be happy to find them and manage the property for you. A management arrangement means you are less likely to fall foul of such arcana as the Furniture and Furnishings (Fire) (Safety) Regulations, which could earn you prosecution by the local trading standards department.

## AND SO TO RETIREMENT

Even if retirement is still a little way off it is worth planning ahead and seeking the middle way between young couples and families moving to the country, who are likely to require a larger property than their previous one, and people who have already retired and may be hoping to trade down profitably. A family house with a detached cottage can have many advantages. Depending on the area, the cottage can be let either long term or as a holiday business – grants may be available for the latter, but planning consent will also be necessary. Selling the house later could provide for a comfortable retirement in the cottage.

Just as buyers of weekend cottages need to be aware of what their requirements really are, so too do people who are retiring.

Once again, different places cater for different needs. As always, it is as well to test your chosen area in winter as well as when it is looking its best.

Cornwall is obviously attractive because of its warm summers and comparatively mild winters, but active people who retire there sometimes need to occupy themselves, perhaps by working part-time or starting a business based on a hobby. Other areas may lack the seductive Cornish climate but the desirability or otherwise of vegetation is something that must be considered in any retirement. For some people, in any part of the country, it is important to have the opportunity to do voluntary or charity work as this keeps them mentally and physically active, and provides company and support. The other side of the coin is the person who has long dreamed of years of sailing, gardening or playing golf, but finds that he or she is not physically up to such activities. It might be wise to have other, contingent, pleasures in mind and choose an area that will also provide these.

Little of this, of course, applies to those happy enough to be able to take a prosperous early retirement. They can settle wherever they wish – or at least wherever their finances allow – although eventually they too will have to look ahead. The need to occupy themselves will probably be more urgent for them than it is for people of retirement age, and they will be less concerned about proximity to facilities. However, it may be that they, too, will move again as they grow older.

For the elderly retired, unless they have the support of a close family or circle of active friends, a country town might very well prove more agreeable than the countryside itself where the possibility of loneliness could be a daunting prospect. In recent years a noticeable factor in property markets like those of Oxford and Cambridge has been the number of people who pass their family homes in the country on to the next generation and buy town flats. In a smaller way, my sister and brother-in-law have sensibly decided on Moreton-in-Marsh for their retirement home, rather than the outlying Cotswold village in which they have lived for a good many years. The move of a few miles to a market town, which is the natural focus of the locality, means they will have all the facilities without cutting themselves off from their present neighbours and friends.

Local services are the most important factor in the choice of a retirement home. The time may come when you can no longer drive, and the easier the walk to shops, post office, church, station and friends the better. The case of the retired teacher who settled in a Victorian rectory 4 miles from the nearest market town illustrates the need to check the existence – or non-existence – of facilities like these before moving. There was no shop in his village and no public transport, except for an erratic market bus once a week. When he took a statutory driving test because of his age, he was refused a licence on the grounds that he had glaucoma – although his condition was no worse than fifteen years before. His wife felt unable to be sole chauffeur for them both, and they had to move away to be near their children, a supermarket and the library.

A sensible precautionary requirement for a retirement home is that it is within convenient reach of good medical attention. Waiting lists for general practitioners and hospitals, and standards of performance, differ from one health authority to the next. Published tables are available, but the statistics are usually a number of years out of date, so it would not be sensible to rely on them too much. For the record, in 1993 general practitioners' lists were longest in Essex, Hertfordshire and Bedfordshire, while the same areas were among the better ones for dentists. It is well worth making sure you know the distance not only to the nearest doctor's surgery, but also the nearest casualty department, and the time the journey is likely to take when the roads are most crowded.

These may seem rather depressing considerations, but knowing that you have checked such things can only add to your sense of comfort and security. In any case, it is to be hoped that the improved quality that you will enjoy as a result of your move will manifest itself in robust mental and physical health.

# CHAPTER THREE

# LISTED PROPERTIES AND PRACTICAL MATTERS

Once you have bought your country home it is likely that you will want to make changes, from updating the kitchen to restoring the fabric, building on an extension or incorporating a granny flat in what was the stable yard. This will almost certainly involve the local planning office. Almost all additions and alterations to the exteriors of existing buildings require planning permission. However, there are circumstances in which certain small extensions and alterations are nodded through, the most important conditions being that a house be a 'single family dwelling', and not subdivided into flats.

If your property is listed there will be further constraints on what you can and cannot do (see below). In a conservation area 'permitted development rights' are also more circumscribed and certain types of cladding, permissible elsewhere, dormer windows and even satellite dishes may need planning permission. However, demolishing a building, or part of a building such as a porch or a chimney stack, which required conservation area consent until 1997, does not currently do so after a House of Lords ruling that demolition of only a part of a building is merely 'alteration', however important its role may be in the character of the area.

One of the first things to do on acquiring a property – or better still, before acquiring it – is therefore to inform yourself about the attitudes of the local authority and any relevant plans that may be in the pipeline. In particular, try to establish a working relationship with the local planning office, if this in any way practicable. Offices and the individuals in them can vary widely in knowledge and helpfulness, but both planning and listing authorities will usually be as helpful as bureaucracy allows. Obviously, the more diplomatic and flexible you can be in approaching them, the better.

# THE GRADE SYSTEM

For many people the comforting response to organizational chaos is to make a list – to be acted upon if one is efficient, to be lost if one is not. As a practical response to the piecemeal destruction of much of the architectural heritage of Britain during the nineteenth century and early parts of the twentieth, the secretaries of state for the environment are required to list buildings of architectural or historic interest. While losses still occur, through ignorance, inefficiency or financial malice, the system generally works well and has played an invaluable part in conserving the architectural heritage of the country.

As a result of the vast national resurvey that has recently been undertaken the total number of listed buildings in England is now nearly half a million. There are also some 15,000 in Wales, 9,000 more in Northern Ireland and about 40,000 in Scotland. Fortunately for anyone who is moving to the country, there is a higher proportion of these buildings in rural areas than in towns, simply because a higher percentage are more than 150 years old. I say fortunately because, despite the planning restraints that worry some potential buyers, the benefits of owning and saving a listed building can be rewarding not only spiritually, but also financially – after all, estate agents would not be so eager to trumpet listed status if it had no bearing on sales. However, the different grades, the protection they give and the degree of inter-ference in the management and disposal of private property they allow for, are not always understood.

In the past owners, purchasers, estate agents, builders, devel-opers and writers on the property market all had to cross their fingers as they plunged into the intricacies of the listing regula-tions: Parliament's first attempt at legislation to protect ancient monuments – but not occupied buildings – had been in 1882, and there had been numerous advances and amendments over the following 110 years. At that point, to the relief of all, the estate agents Jackson-Stops & Staff, together with Simmons & Simmons, a law firm with specialist property, planning and devel-opment departments, published a layman's guide to listed building legislation.

This guide, which has since been joined by a more basic intro-ductory pamphlet, *Listed Buildings and Conservation Areas*, and a second guide dealing with insuring listed buildings and their contents (see Chapter Five and Directory, page 229), is essential reading for anyone who is thinking of buying a listed property. There are currently three grades – I, II* and II (A, B and C in Scotland) – which were set up in 1948, but while the listing itself is now a matter of law, the grades are not. Rather, they are an administrative convenience.

Just 2 per cent of English structures are listed Grade I, 'of exceptional interest', with about 4 per cent listed Grade II*, 'particularly important and of more than special interest'. The remainder, at Grade II, are deemed 'of special interest, warranting every effort to preserve them'. I say 'structures' because not only houses, but almost anything except the entirely subterranean, including ice houses, sundials, dovecotes, horse troughs, mile-stones lychgates and even headstones may be listed. Essentially, all pre-1700 and most pre-1840 buildings in anything like their original condition should be listed, as are many major Victorian, Edwardian structures and some of the best inter-war examples. A thirty-year rule, introduced fairly recently, gives the possibility of protection to any 1950s building, and an emergency procedure for threatened contemporary structures.

It must be emphasized that once a building is listed it is not just the exterior that is subject to regulation. One of the most common causes of conflict is the removal or insertion of interior walls, often when converting bedrooms to bathrooms – as in the case of a senior partner in a London law firm who had to apply for retrospective consents for nineteen bathrooms in his listed country property. Essentially, alterations without consent are undertaken at the owner's peril.

Another area of contention is the curtilege – the outbuildings and surrounding areas that form part of the character of a property. In effect, all are deemed to be listed and this includes surviving structures incorporated in new buildings, for example in stable yards, when large houses are divided up.

Listing by no means always prevents demolition or destructive alteration, but it does usually ensure that nothing is done in haste and nowadays, as the former minister Teresa Gorman found with her Essex porch, the courts are often willing to give the regulations teeth. As a representative of the Ancient Monuments Society put it: 'Ignorance is no defence in English law. All in all, a civilized owner will find that the rules should not affect his life at all, except to his benefit.'

Despite the resurvey mentioned earlier, some important houses have managed to evade the notice of the authorities. This can lead to tragedies from the heritage point of view, but on occasions it can also allow sense and sensitivity to prevail over an unimaginative insistence on going by the book. For example, because a fascinating late-eighteenth century house had inexplicably avoided listing, its owner was able to remove various nineteenth-century accretions from the interiors to reveal something like the original form, without having to face the wrath of the Victorian Society.

On the other hand, the case of the site of the Globe Theatre on London's Bankside is a wonderful example of rules that were meant to protect and enhance the heritage but actually militated against it. Because a dull Regency terrace above part of the site is listed, Shakespeare's own theatre cannot be fully uncovered.

# RESPONSIBILITIES AND RESTRICTIONS

There can be tremendous kudos in owning a listed building, but naturally there is also a responsibility. You must expect restrictions on what you can and cannot do with your own property. Before buying it might be sensible to check, for instance, whether any or all of the interior decoration is listed. Even though it may be 'important', it might not be to your taste, and you will have to decide whether this outweighs what you like about the house.

Remember that, regardless of your property's grade, all alterations that will affect the character of the house will require listed building consent. The Planning (Listed Buildings and Conservation Areas) Act, 1990, section 7, states clearly: 'No person shall execute or cause to be executed any works for the demolition of a listed building or for its alteration or extension in any manner which would affect its character as a building of special architectural or historic interest, unless the works are authorised.'

For this reason, it is always sensible to check whether consent is required for any alterations you may wish to make. The planning authority's conservation officer, if there is one, will advise you. Otherwise contact English Heritage, the appropriate amenity society or a consultant expert in listed buildings.

An illegal alteration lays not only the owner but also the building contractor open to prosecution, fines and ultimately imprisonment. More probably, the owner will be required to restore the building to its former state. The old ploy of allowing a listed structure to become dangerous, so as to be able to demolish it, is supposedly countered by an 'urgent works notice' from the local authority. This can only be served on unoccupied parts of a building, but may eventually be followed by compulsory purchase. However, these powers are cumbersome in operation, and all too frequently ineffective in practice.

It is also worth remembering that you can actually be penalized because of errors on the part of the listing authorities. On occasions it may not be clear that a property is in fact listed, because of a misdescription in the listing or, perhaps, because the name of the property has been changed. Even then, it will be deemed to be your fault if you inadvertently breach the regulations. And if a previous owner has made alterations that are subsequently ruled to be unacceptable, it is the present owner who must put them right. Luckily, however, occurrences like these are rare.

If your house is listed as Grade I or Grade II* you can apply to various bodies, from English Heritage to parish councils, for grants (see Directory, page 230); and even owners of Grade II properties will be listened to sympathetically. But wait until you have actually bought the house before applying. Applications for grants from existing owners will be more readily considered than if they come from prospective purchasers. This is because the promise of a grant could allow the vendor to put his price up without benefiting the property.

If an extension or outbuilding is an eyesore you can demolish it without consent provided it was added after 1 July 1948. Alterations and extensions to listed buildings may be exempt from VAT. Repairs, however, are not. Although both planning and listed building consent must be applied for, there is only one fee. Unfortunately council tax, which was not formerly levied on such properties, now applies.

I would urge anyone who has bought, or is contemplating buying, a listed property to keep the Jackson-Stops guide within easy reach. Among other things it defines listing and its implications, and will lead you through the procedures for applying for consent and appealing against rejection.

Finally, never, ever, be tempted into making a joke or even a light-hearted comment in your dealings with planning and listing authorities. Careful owners who replaced a rotten bathroom window in their Grade II house in Powys did so immaculately, and when it was painted the new work was quite indistinguishable from the old. They laughingly pointed this out to a grading official who was making a tour of inspection, and incurred a telling-off for having omitted to apply for permission. They were lucky not to have to remove the new window and reinstate the old one.

## ALTERATIONS AND IMPROVEMENTS

Whether your property is listed or not, alterations that will cause disturbance should ideally be accomplished before you move in, and that may include a new heating system. Installing anything in the way of piping and drainage – and wiring for new communications and technology – is likely to be cheaper and more practical before you plaster, paper or decorate. I should probably have mentioned this much earlier in the book, but here, at last, is rule number one for anyone moving to the country: buy more bedding. Almost inevitably your new home will be colder than the one you are used to, especially at night. The change of temperature can be even more of a shock to visiting friends from town, so stock up on sheets and blankets. You may find that you don't need a new heating system after all.

However, if you do need to change the system, make sure you get the new one right. This is vital, not only for your future comfort, but also for your future budget. Cold naturally seems a pressing problem to new inhabitants of old houses, but take the time to think through any system carefully; and take local advice before committing yourself to a particular fuel.

The coldest house I have ever stayed in was a castle in Ireland. In the nineteenth century a wonderfully efficient system had been devised whereby turf from the nearby bog was brought by conveyor belt into a central area, whence it could be distributed by lift to the various floors, unseen by the gentry. This was splendid until the government nationalized the bogs. The compensation they paid allowed the then owner of the castle to install a thoroughly up-to-date oil-fired system – which almost immediately became too expensive to operate except as an occasional luxury, thanks to the 1970s oil crisis. It was difficult to sleep, even with overcoats, copious quantities of sloe gin and a small electric fire.

The point of this tale is that oil is comparatively cheap once again, although the cost is on the rise, and is the preferred heating of many people in the countryside, especially where mains gas is not available. The owner of that castle is no doubt now snug, and saving on his sloe gin. However, oil requires a very large tank, and oil prices have been known to change dramatically. Gas central heating is probably the most inexpensive, convenient and straightforward system, provided it is laid on in your area and can be piped straight to your house.

Oil and gas are really the only two options as coal is no longer economical for heating houses other than in an open fire. While this may be a beautiful thing, it does not always give the greatest heat – and coal requires storage space as well as regular trips to the coal hole. It is intriguing to conjecture that these staples of twentieth-century heating will be out of date by the end of another century (see 'A Vision of the Country AD 2097', opposite).

## BUILDERS AND BUILDINGS

Whatever other alterations and improvements you wish to carry out – assuming that you have threaded your way through the Slough of Planning and the Thickets of Listing – you are likely to

# A Vision of the Country AD 2097

DAVID FLEMING

The solution to the energy problem of the next century is not to generate more, but to think of ways of making do with less. This is not the usual stuff of futurology – it is the day-to-day graft of applying energy-saving technology and living in ways which are less dependent on energy. It is probable that, early in the century, all new houses will be built so that they do not need to buy any power for space-heating, and older houses will begin to be fitted up to those standards. Cooking will use less energy, partly through better technology, and partly by energy-saving methods, such as slow-cooking and more use of microwaves. Lighting and refrigeration will become more efficient, but even with these savings, households will be under pressure to use the minimum amounts, in order to stay within the limits of supply available to them.

Under these circumstances, local self-reliance could be rediscovered. Local communities will have the incentive to generate much of their own power, and to co-operate in methods of saving it. The principle of 'do-it-yourself' will develop strongly. In some ways, this is a continuation of a long trend since the low point of self-sufficiency by small households in the mid-nineteenth century. Scrooge, in Dickens' *A Christmas Carol*, met local poor householders on Christmas morning carrying their prepared goose round to the baker's oven for cooking; since then, households have brought cooking, clothes-washing, entertainment – everything they can – into their own houses. The supply of energy will join that trend, but conservation will be a critical part of the solution. It could be that, to the household of 2100, the energy market of the late twentieth century – when you simply had to flick a switch to obtain unlimited supplies of cheap energy, and when everyone in Britain was able to travel an average of 6,000 miles a year by road – will seem as long ago as Scrooge's Christmas morning seems to us.

find yourself in the hands of a local builder, and must hope that he turns out to be the Giant Steadfast rather than the Ogre Despair. With luck he will come wreathed in personal recommendations from experienced neighbours, and all will be well.

In turn he will find carpenters, plumbers and other necessary craftsmen, all of whom should be fluent in the local building vernacular. This can be important if you are to avoid potentially dangerous anachronisms. For instance, a seventeenth- or eighteenth-century cottage was probably built without what a modern architect would consider to be foundations. If, in accordance with modern wisdom, you insert a thick concrete base you will prevent the natural movement of the structure that has allowed the building to react, organically as it were, to changing physical and climatic conditions over several hundred years. A traditionally built house can breathe and move as it needs to, without danger of collapse. If you restrain it, it may very well break. Alas, such inherited knowledge, which has proved itself by the test of time, is not always trusted by builders and architects, especially in this age of quick construction and the breeze block.

In places like National Parks there are fierce regulations as to what you can and cannot do to your house and its surroundings (see Chapter Four), but even if your property is not in one of these areas it will demand its own individual treatment. The work of Lutyens is chiefly associated with Surrey, but a Lutyens house is very obviously by Lutyens, whether it is in Suffolk or Surrey. No one would try to force one of them into the mould of Suffolk plaster and thatch, just because it happened to be in East Anglia.

## CESSPITS

Many country properties do not have main drainage, so it may be necessary to become an initiate in the mysteries of the cesspit. If you have to construct one, find an experienced builder who will instruct you in the traditional practices. If there is a cesspit on the property, check with the vendor that it functions well, and also check on the whereabouts and efficiency of cesspits belonging to neighbours. Seepage from next door into a low-lying part of your garden would be unwelcome.

One of the most common causes of malfunction in drainage and sewerage systems is the use of the wrong detergents, which fur up the arteries in a cholesterol-like manner. Similarly, only white lavatory paper should be used because coloured dyes do terrible things to the beneficial bacteria. When it comes to cesspits there is no substitute for local knowledge and experience.

# CHAPTER FOUR

# NATIONAL PARKS, THE NATIONAL TRUST AND UNUSUAL PROPERTIES

For the population at large the National Parks and the National Trust are among the true glories of England and Wales. Naturally enough in a democracy both have their critics, but our own and future generations would be very much the poorer without them. They have prevented much sublime natural beauty and many magnificent human achievements from being destroyed for ever. It is, however, sometimes easy for visitors to consider both landscapes and buildings as theme parks or museums rather than real places in which people live and work. Equally, people who live in National Parks or rent National Trust properties must be prepared to make some compromises between the freedom to do as they wish with their property, and the general good.

There are plenty of meritorious structures that are not important enough to concern the Trust, and are financially impossible for local or other heritage bodies. However, since the 1970s more and more people have become aware of what individuals can do to supplement the efforts of official organizations in preserving the architectural heritage of the country. Conservation, restoration and conversion are now, thank heavens, more likely reactions to ruinous or redundant buildings than demolition. Thanks to the Society for the Protection of Ancient Buildings, SAVE Britain's Heritage and other campaigners there is now plenty of information and support for people who venture to become saviours of buildings at risk.

Obviously there will be planning and other conditions to be met, and remember too that if you buy a property in one of the National Parks, or lease one from a large estate, such as the Crown, the Duchy of Cornwall or an organization like the National Trust, you will find that you are subject to regulations, conditions and restraints which would not obtain elsewhere. Areas of Outstanding Natural Beauty also have their own constraints. It is important to be aware of these before you buy.

# NATIONAL PARKS

There are currently eleven National Parks in England and Wales, each looked after by an authority composed of representatives of local councils and specialist appointees of the secretary of state for the environment. They cover large tracts of Northumberland, the Lake District, Yorkshire Dales, North York Moors, the Peak District, Snowdonia, the Broads, the Pembrokeshire coast, Brecon Beacons, Exmoor and Dartmoor. Two more are shortly to be set up: the New Forest and South Downs. They do not win universal approbation, as the reaction of the Country Landowners' Association to the announcement of the new parks in September 1999 testified.

In its view, the announcement would 'do nothing to make the countryside any more available to anyone – it will merely add an unnecessary level of bureaucracy to an already overburdened countryside community ... A solution would have been to have properly funded the conservation bodies and local authorities already managing these areas, rather than siphoning money into another layer of bureaucracy.'

Although the authorities maintain that they 'neither have nor seek absolute power', preferring to work in partnership with local residents, organizations and councils, and with representatives of groups such as ramblers, they do indeed hold very considerable sway over the lives of people living within their boundaries. They all provide booklets of rules and conditions. The examples given here are all taken from Dartmoor, but they will be very similar in all the Parks.

A first point to note is the legal definition of 'development' as 'the carrying out of building, engineering, mining or other operations in, on, over or under land, or the making of any material change in use of any buildings or other land' is a lawyer's paradise: almost every word is the subject of further interpretation or definition.

For the record, works of maintenance, improvement or other alterations that only affect the interior of a building or do not materially affect its external appearance are not development. However, it is important to remember that many buildings within National Parks are listed and require listed building consent. There are some 2,500 within the Dartmoor park alone. It should also be noted that within the Dartmoor park special permission is necessary to clad any part of even an unlisted dwelling house with 'stone, artificial stone, timber, plastic or tiles' – but is unnecessary, apparently, if the owner uses other materials or enlarges the building by an addition, such as a dormer window, to its roof. If you run a bed and breakfast establishment or a farm shop, you will wish to announce the business, but will need permission to display 'any word, letter, model, sign, placard, board, notice, device or representation, whether illuminated or not, in the nature of, and employed wholly or partly for the purposes of advertisement, announcement or direction ...'

It makes good sense to check with the planning officer to see if permission is likely to be required before carrying out any alterations that might be construed as development. Unexpectedly, you do not actually have to submit an application before development takes place, although it is wise to do so. There are lengthy and involved procedures whereby the authority can get rid of any alterations that have been made and are subsequently deemed unacceptable. Mechanisms exist whereby a disappointed applicant can appeal to the secretary of state later if permission is refused.

Most applications have to be accompanied by a fee. However, the Dartmoor authority's built environment service not only advises on architectural design and conservation matters, but helps owners of listed buildings with a grant scheme for authentic repairs and restoration. The farm and countryside service offers farm conservation scheme grants for work which is not, or is insufficiently, grant-aided by national schemes.

# NATIONAL TRUST PROPERTIES

If you would prefer to rent rather than buy it is worth considering a National Trust property. Obviously the great country houses are not on offer but the Trust owns many other buildings, from dower houses to stable-yard flats and cottages on estates, and not all are needed by estate workers or the Trust's staff. There are two types of tenancy: about fifty custodial tenancies, which come with curatorial responsibilities and involve allowing the public certain levels of access to the property; and estate houses and cottages without public access, which may be let on long or short leases. Details are available from the relevant regional offices, which can be contacted through the National Trust's head office (see Directory, page 230).

Many more people enquire about National Trust tenancies than could ever be accommodated, and your suitability for any vacancy will be assessed as carefully as you assess the suitability of the property to your needs. This applies particularly if you are interested in becoming a custodial tenant, as responsibilities vary according to the property. The Trust looks for people who are sympathetic to its aims in caring for places of historic interest or natural beauty and making them accessible. They also need to be prepared to offer a welcome to visitors on days when a property is open – and will have to balance this with personal circumstances, such as bringing up a family. Rents are to some extent negotiable, but both custodial and other tenants must be able to offer a rent that is in line with the market price for the type of property they are interested in.

Ian Homersham, former joint chairman of the estate agents John D. Wood, has lived in Trust properties since 1973. Currently he and his wife have the home farmhouse on the Coleshill estate in Berkshire. Most of the inhabitants of the village work for the Trust on the estate and in nearby Buscot, and the agent's office is next door to the farmhouse. This means that the Homershams are under the eye of their landlord but, equally, they can get things done very quickly if need be.

The lease stipulates that the building's fabric is the responsibility of the Trust, but windows, wiring, heating and the interior are the tenant's – under permission. For instance, there is a stipulation that the property be repainted every five years, and only specific colours are allowed. Ian Homersham is not polite about the 'sort of milk chocolate' used on garage and other doors. Garden developments, trees and hedges are also carefully supervised, and it was by no means easy for him to win his campaign to put a swimming pool in a small and completely secluded enclosure that had once housed a brick boiler room for the greenhouses.

'So many tenants are quick to complain,' Ian Homersham says. 'They don't readily acknowledge their good fortune. We have always found the Trust and their agents to be extremely considerate landlords. Indeed, a few years ago I enquired about buying a long lease for my future security. As it happened they refused, because this house is at the core of the estate and they were uncomfortable with the thought that the lease could be sold on to someone of whom they didn't approve. It can be done with less sensitive places.'

# CHALLENGES
# AND CONVERSIONS

Every Englishman's home is his castle, and even today some castles are also Englishmen's homes, as are other quirky buildings such as windmills, oast houses, barns, farm outbuildings, redundant churches, former schoolhouses and follies of all descriptions. A picturesque but not too ruinous ruin can bring out the romantic white knight in anyone. You have only to buy it for a song and, under the ardent attentions of your restoring zeal, the princess will awake and beauty bloom again. Or so it might seem.

Converting a building, let alone bringing a ruin back from the dead, can be a Herculean task and before the dream fades, or your finances crumble into dust, take a cool look at what you might be taking on. In 1979 it cost very little comparatively to take on a decrepit farmhouse that faced on to one of the snaking main streets of the Suffolk wool town of Lavenham. It would be interesting, thought its buyers, to do it up a bit while running a business from home. Nearly twenty years later those buyers knew that their whole lives had become bound up in the unending resuscitation of what was in fact a quite remarkable timber-framed merchant's house of the thirteenth century. By then it was listed Grade I, the owners were uncovering ever more features, including wall paintings, and they felt they needed to retire. But with what satisfaction. They had resuscitated a national treasure.

Some old buildings are past help, few are straightforward, but many can indeed be saved and given new lives. 'Feasibility Studies for Redundant Historic Buildings' appeared in the 1999 edition of *The Building Conservation Directory* (see Directory, page 232), an essential purchase for anyone attempting to do up a period building – or indeed a building of any sort. It is primarily directed at surveyors, and several urban examples are instanced, but private individuals will find it equally useful, and in general the principles apply in the country as well as in towns. It may also be useful as an introduction to the ways in which surveyors' minds work.

All kinds of unusual properties are available for resuscitation or conversion and this book deals with some of the more popular ones. However, whether a building is a watermill or a windmill, a stable or a barn, the basic guidelines remain the same. In particular, in many cases it would be unthinkable to take on the task without respecting the character and original function of the structure. There is not much point in living in a former church if you turn the interior into a series of box-like rooms that could be in a 1960s block of flats. Luckily there are sources of specialist advice, some of which are discussed at the end of this chapter, while others are listed in the Directory.

# BARNS AND FARM BUILDINGS

One type of building that needs particular sensitivity if it is to be turned into something other than itself is the traditional barn. Whether wooden or stone, it was generally built without windows and when it is converted into a dwelling the whole character of the exterior can be shattered by fenestration. In times of agricultural difficulty it is natural that farmers should attempt asset-stripping operations, and the barn is often seen as a realizable asset.

There is, of course, nothing new about farm buildings becoming redundant, nor about converting them for different uses. In the past farmers either left them to decay or adapted them to meet changing contemporary needs – in 1810 the great agricultural writer Arthur Young commented that Suffolk barns were 'uselessly large'. Until comparatively recently, however, it was unusual to recycle them for residential use.

Over the last decade the position has changed considerably. In 1987–8 there were more applications to demolish barns than any other category of listed building. Together with miscellaneous farm buildings they accounted for one-fifth of the total. Many more disappeared because they were unlisted and their demolition was therefore unrecorded. Furthermore, there was little control over those which were converted to residential or other use. They were simply 'delisted', and developers did much as they wished, often destroying their character.

In 1988 SAVE published a report by Gillian Darley entitled *A Future for Farm Buildings*. Anyone tempted to try a conversion should try to find a copy. Even though the world has moved on and some of the information is out of date, the general principles, and excellent illustrations of both good and bad conversions, are instructive.

In October 1999 the Countryside Agency came out against what it termed 'barn blight', and part-funded a good-taste guide to avoid the painful conversions of previous decades when a medieval barn could sprout television aerials and roof lights, dormer windows and picture windows, concrete patches, do-it-yourself extensions and PVC tatters. The guide was devised by Steve Roderick, the countryside officer for the Chilterns Area of Outstanding Natural Beauty, which explains the booklet's title: *Chilterns Buildings Design Guide*. It has far more than local application.

Steve Roderick offers a simple rule of thumb: 'If you've got a conversion wrong, it looks like suburbia. If you've got it right, it looks as if it has always been there.' As with other conversions, there is no point in embarking on the task if you are going to deny the original purpose of the building. A barn is supposed to have large open spaces inside, and should not be divided into boxes. Similarly, you must accept that there will be dark, or at least dim, corners.

Planners in some areas will not put barns on the 'at risk' register in case they attract unsuitable converters. If they do, even the fact that 77,296 English farm buildings – including more barns than schools, stations or pubs – are listed may not protect them. On the other hand, it would be tragically foolish if all redundant farm buildings were allowed to collapse because suitable people were being turned away.

In the autumn of 1999 the Banbury office of FPDSavills issued a series of guidelines to farmers thinking of converting barns and other redundant buildings. The following points will be relevant if you are thinking of buying such conversions, or intend to convert a farm building yourself.

◆ Try to retain control if you are planning to subdivide a barn that is close to a farmhouse. An outright sale might affect your house's future value, and there can be no guarantee that new neighbours will be pleasant.
◆ You will require planning permission and this will probably entail costs and delays.
◆ Check whether construction traffic will affect the surrounding property, and whether the Highways Agency has any concerns over access to the road.
◆ Take professional advice if you intend letting. Be aware that immediate costs will be high, and the payback period may be a few years.
◆ Don't overlook VAT or you may not be able to recover the costs of conversion.

# SCHOOLHOUSES

Victorian and Edwardian village schoolhouses can make excellent homes. Because they usually consist of one large, high schoolroom with several much smaller rooms at one end, they are particularly attractive to writers, musicians and artists. A gallery can often be inserted, and it is sometimes possible to make discreet additions to the building. Unfortunately for do-it-yourself converters, the majority of the most desirable school buildings were sold off some years ago and are already serving new purposes, while many remaining village schools are either unlikely to close or are housed in more recent buildings which are less suitable for conversion. On the other hand, they may have large playgrounds. This is not always the case with older schools – pupils played on the village green – so these may not provide much of an opportunity to create a garden.

## CHURCHES AND CHAPELS

Former rectories and vicarages are at the top of the housing market in terms of popularity and the Church Commissioners must have disturbed nights as they contemplate the prices now made by the houses they have sold since the 1960s. In one village I know well the moated 'Old Rectory', which has medieval origins and comes with a large garden and a couple of fields, recently resold for well over £1 million, while the 1960s no-nonsense brick 'Former Rectory' which replaced it and has been in lay hands for the last decade, is also now worth about £300,000.

Although the rectories and vicarages have gone, as parishes become joint ministries and some congregations wither, there are occasional opportunities to buy a redundant church or chapel for conversion to residential use. By no means all churches are suitable, but the relevant Church of England bodies do all in their power to avoid the demolition of buildings of any historic interest or architectural merit. These authorities include the Council for the Care of Churches, which has statutory oversight of all alterations and disposals of church property; the Advisory Board for Redundant Churches, which advises on buildings of architectural, historical and archaeological interest; and the Diocesan Redundant Churches Uses committees.

*New Uses for Redundant Churches* is a simple pamphlet, available from the Church Commissioners (see Directory, page 234), that takes prospective purchasers through the process of acquiring and converting churches for domestic use or for other uses such as offices, museums and sports or arts and crafts centres. If you have no particular building in mind, but like the idea of converting a church, the commissioners have a list of what is available, and will tell you which agents they are using. If a deal seems likely they will prepare a draft redundancy and conversion scheme in consultation with you. This will be open to public objections and will usually remove the legal effects of consecration. Next come planning and, probably, listing consents.

A number of special conditions are, naturally, attached to church conversions. These usually include covenants that ensure the property is used only for authorized purposes, in order to protect it from unauthorized alterations or demolition and to reassure the neighbours, as well to allow public access to any remaining graves at agreed times and protect against the disturbance of any human remains. As a general rule the law requires these to be reburied elsewhere when a church is converted, but the Home Office may grant an exemption if your proposals involve no disturbance. Tombstones are usually either left in place or removed before completion, and all the buildings' contents are removed except by special arrangement. The commissioners should sort out rights of way, and the public's 'church-going' rights lapse with deconsecration.

There is no central organization to apply to if you want to convert a redundant Nonconformist chapel. These tend to be placed on the market through local agents on an *ad hoc* basis. The regulations regarding burials are the same, but Methodists have been known to add a covenant banning the consumption of alcohol in their former chapels. Church-warming parties may be a little more exuberant.


## CASTLES AND COUNTRY HOUSES

In a hundred years' time architectural historians may look back on Kit Martin as one of the most important figures of our day. Since the

1970s he has been responsible not just for the preservation of many large country houses which might otherwise have been destroyed, but for giving them new life and purpose. His influence and example have led many other developers to take on such buildings and adapt them to modern residential needs, rather than demolishing them so that their sites can be covered with newly built housing.

The secret discovered by Kit Martin is that in many cases even the whitest of elephants can be dissected without the destruction of either its architectural purity or its essential character. By subdividing, several manageable homes can be made from one country house. In the eighteenth-century heyday of country house living, buildings such as Burley on the Hill in Rutland, or Wardour Castle, Wiltshire, would have housed a population equivalent to that of several of the surrounding villages. Carefully divided into individual houses and apartments suitable for modern families of various sizes, they can do so again. Great rooms are preserved, although the original flow between them is inevitably often lost; staircases may have to be discreetly inserted along with bathrooms and kitchens – but the houses live again.

Generally each portion is allocated a suitable area of private garden, while other parts of the grounds are communally owned and maintained. In some cases a hall or particular stateroom is also held communally, and can be used for cultural events or parties. This is a way in which many more people can enjoy an adapted form of the country house lifestyle, without having either the responsibilities of a great house and estate, or the trials and expense of converting or restoring for themselves. There is also the security of neighbours and the communally employed caretakers, handymen and gardeners.

# THATCHED BUILDINGS

Thatched houses and cottages belong to a group that is almost too large to be considered unusual in any way. There are about

50,000 thatched properties in the United Kingdom (and rather more than 1,000 thatchers) – but potential owners will be faced with challenges and satisfactions that do not concern people who live beneath roofs of other kinds.

Thatch is a wonderful material that provides the perfect insulation, ensuring that a house is cool in summer and warm in winter, and greatly enhances the quality of life, 'provided, that is, you are not an arachnophobe,' according to Andrew Newman, who lived in a rose-covered thatched cottage in Nether Wallop, Hampshire, for seven years. 'We had some really big beasts who evidently found it as comfortable as we did.'

Regional styles of thatch differ and are partly the product of different indigenous materials. Norfolk reed, for example, is the most durable and a water-reed thatch can last seventy years. Wheat reed is characteristic of the south-west of the country, and combed wheat thatch may be expected to last from thirty to forty years. Straw thatch has a life of between fifteen and twenty years. These lifespans assume good original workmanship, periodic reridging and maintenance as required.

Would-be buyers of thatched properties, which can be substantial as well as cottage-sized – there is even a castle in Dorset – should remember that most are listed at least Grade II. This means that local authorities will not give consent for the decorative style of a roof to be altered. Before buying it is wise to check on close or overhanging trees and make sure that the roof is free of parasitic vegetation.

It might be assumed that the cost of insurance would be prohibitive but the extra £50 or even £100 a year is not much in the scale of things. Furthermore, insuring a thatched property in a traditional thatch area often costs less than insuring one that is isolated in a sea of tiles because everyone in the neighbourhood will be careful about bonfires, barbecues and similar hazards. The risk of fire has in fact decreased in recent years as a result of central heating and because some authorities insist on the insertion of half-hour fire-resistant boarding or a similar skin beneath rethatched roofs. Obviously, you would never use, or allow builders to use, a blowlamp or hot-air stripper near the property.

Other precautions include making sure the loft area is free of draughts, and clearing the under-roof of any cobwebs – which are extremely inflammable. Also remove any combustible rubbish and, most of all, pay special attention to the chimney. It is a potential fire hazard if not kept in good order as sparks can penetrate to the roof by way of cracks or breaks in the mortar. It should be swept at least twice a year.

On leaving their thatched cottage Mr Newman's daughter could not sleep for some while because of a previously unheard noise: the rattle of rain on a tiled roof.


# SAVIOURS

Anyone who is serious about taking on the challenge of saving a building at risk can find out more from the Society for the Protection of Ancient Buildings (SPAB) and from SAVE Britain's Heritage. The SPAB provides its members with a list of buildings at risk that are for sale. There is a huge variety at any one time, from castles to cottages, throughout the country and priced at anything from a few thousand to several million pounds. English Heritage publishes a *Buildings at Risk Register*, but only Grade I and II* buildings are included and these are not necessarily for sale. Local council registers include Grade II as well. Another body which advises on practical matters and, importantly, funding is the Architectural Heritage Fund.

Many sources of practical advice can be found in *The Building Conservation Directory* and the Royal Institute of Chartered Surveyors can often help with others. Local planning officers, English Heritage, the National Trust and the various preservation groups such as the Victorian Society have registers of approved specialists and craftsmen. Should none of these come up with what you need, both Historic Scotland and the Irish

Department of Environment and Local Government have produced a series of booklets of conservation guidelines which cover all sorts of topics from windows, lime, plasterwork, mortars, pointing and renders, rising damp and timber decay, stone walling and ironwork to fire precautions, security and maintenance. The booklets may be obtained from Historic Scotland or the Irish Georgian Society. All the sources given above are in the Directory (pages 229-236).

# Feasibility Studies for Redundant Historic Buildings

There are thousands of old buildings throughout the country which are empty or redundant. In an unoccupied building, the chance of somebody spotting a leak in time is remote, and for the vast majority of historic buildings, redundancy inevitably leads to decay. The Buildings at Risk Survey published by English Heritage lists 1,500 historic buildings at risk in England alone.

Taking on a redundant historic building may seem a daunting task, but the opportunities for imaginative purchasers with courage are enormous – and there are few things more satisfying or rewarding for people who love old buildings than direct action.

However, buying and conserving an old building inevitably entails an element of risk. Old buildings deteriorate by complex mechanisms, which will remain a mystery to those without specialist expertise, and even specialists can be caught out. Project costs can rise after work has commenced on site, so too can interest rates – and property values can fall. Success is made more likely by effective risk management, but like any property transaction, some element of uncertainty almost invariably remains from start to finish.

One alternative to buying a property yourself, is to set up a building preservation trust which protects individual members from liability. As a not-for-profit organisation with charitable status, a building preservation trust can access wider sources of finance than private individuals can, through fund-raising and grants such as the Heritage Lottery Fund, and the Landfill Tax Credit Scheme.

Although there are over 150 BPTs in England, they still remain thin on the ground, and most can tackle only one project at a time. There is a need for more preservation trusts to be established, particularly in areas were numerous historic buildings are at risk.

## IS CONSERVATION FEASIBLE?

Whether you choose to purchase a redundant building privately, or through a buildings preservation trust, it is vital that you know as much as possible about the building you would like to buy, and that your requirements can be met by the building within the conditions imposed by its character and interest, your budget and the requirements of the authorities. A thorough feasibility study is therefore an essential prerequisite, even though it may seem expensive and time consuming, and it may result in the project being abandoned.

A good feasibility study includes six components, which address key questions as set out below.

### 1 The survey: is the structure viable?

The aim of the survey is to assess the condition of the building and if there are faults, to identify their cause. It is the first, and arguably the most important, element of risk management, so it should be carried out by a professional who specialises in conservation work, such as a surveyor accredited in conservation by the RICS. The structural problems of historic buildings can be highly complex and are often caused by the inappropriate use of modern repair methods and the misdiagnosis of faults in the past. Treating the symptom of decay or structural damage without understanding its cause can lead to unnecessary treatment, recurrence of the fault immediately afterwards, and in some cases an incorrect repair may actually cause damage.

A full structural survey may seem relatively expensive, but buying an old building without one can be an expensive gamble. The results of the survey may also provide a useful tool for negotiating an appropriate sale price.

### 2 Use options: what will the market support?

Under normal circumstances, for a project to be financially viable, its costs (including the cost of purchasing, repairing and adapting the building) should not exceed the value or 'resale' value of the building after the work is completed.

The use of the building may have a significant impact on its resale value. For example, a building by a busy main road may be less attractive as a house than a similar property in a quiet side street, but may be more attractive as commercial premises or offices dependent on passing trade. However, calculating the resale value of a well conserved building with historic character can be difficult if there are no similar properties on the market, and interesting conversions frequently buck existing trends. For example, 15 years ago hardly anyone lived in the centre of Manchester and most of the big Victorian warehouses which dominate much of the city centre were under-used or redundant. Now warehouse conversions in cities like Manchester are highly fashionable and loft-style apartments command a premium. Bear in mind that the value of a building is whatever somebody is prepared to pay for it, not necessarily what an estate agent thinks it is worth.

## 3 Local authority requirements: what alterations will be accepted?

Three local authority departments are most likely to have an interest in the conversion or alteration of an existing building: Planning, Building Control, and Highways. The main issues are planning, listed building and conservation requirements (see Chapter 3). Traffic generation and car parking requirements may also be critical where a change in use requires planning permission and is likely to generate more traffic. Fire safety issues may also present problems for a conversion.

## 4 The preliminary design scheme: what facilities will the building provide?

The first aim of the preliminary design is to explore alternative schemes which satisfy the needs of the building and the client without unduly compromising the character and historic interest of the building.

To ensure that the design reflects your requirements and avoids wasting time, it is essential to produce a brief for the architect or designer to work to. This should summarise the conservation require-ments including the aspects of its character and history which must be safeguarded, the use of materials and details, and the treatment of the existing fabric. It should also describe the proposed use of the building, the facilities required and any particular attributes which you consider to be important.

The brief should also detail the services you wish your consultant to provide after the building has been purchased so that the consultant can prepare an estimate of his or her services to be included in your analysis.

## 5 Financial summary: what will the project cost?

Once a preliminary design has been prepared it is possible to prepare a draft budget and cash flow forecast to identify how much money will be required and when.

The budget will need to take into account the acquisition costs (including the purchase price as well as all related fees such as profes-sional, legal and mortgage fees), consultants' fees (including the survey, feasibility study, investigation and recording, design, structural engineering and contract management among others), building works (including the work identified by the survey and all conservation and repair work) as well as a contingency sum for the unforeseen.

## 6 Sources of finance: who will fund a ruin?

For a private purchaser the usual source of financial assistance is a bank loan or mortgage. In either case the organisation making the investment will need to be sure that the purchaser is able to meet their interest charges and repayments and that the building represents sound collateral. 'High street' banks and building societies are often reluctant to lend money for the purchase and improvement of a redun-dant building, and may impose stringent conditions. Furthermore, the valuation surveys required by these lenders are very rarely carried out by a specialist in historic building work, and some requirements may be completely inappropriate for an historic building. Some shopping around will be necessary to find an institution which will consider the property and which will be prepared to accept a survey by an independent but suitably qualified surveyor.

Cadw, English Heritage, the Environment and Heritage Service (DoE Northern Ireland) and Historic Scotland offer grants for conservation work but these are generally targeted at the most important listed buildings and owners with the greatest need. A project involving a redundant listed building stands a good chance of success, particularly if it is at risk and the project can be shown to be unviable without the grant. Local authorities are also able to make grants for the repair and maintenance of historic buildings, including buildings in conservation areas. However, some local authorities are hard-pressed to make any grants at all.

## GENERAL

Consider each element of the feasibility study carefully and work out how each one can be instigated. If it seems likely that the result of one simple element, such as the availability of a key grant, will rule out the proposal, give that element the highest priority.

Programme each element so that the feasibility study period does not become unnecessarily drawn out, but do not allow yourself to be rushed into a decision either, as mistakes can be very expensive, particularly where historic buildings are concerned.

Finally, when you are entirely satisfied that you can achieve an acceptable scheme within the financial constraints, you can proceed to make a formal offer to purchase the property.

Your offer should reflect the resale value of the building once any essential work has been carried out, less the cost of the work. If this figure is lower than the value suggested by the estate agent, the building owners are more likely to accept your offer if it is backed by figures which show the true cost of essential refurbishment works.

# CHAPTER FIVE

# SECURITY AND INSURANCE

If you read the newspapers, especially during the summer months, it is easy to believe that the countryside is infested with burglars, that village greens are full of idle youths who hang about hoping to happen on someone to mug and that every weekend the cowed centres of market towns are filled with mindless drug fiends and drunken rioters.

In April 1998 detailed crime statistics were issued by the Home Office. These agreed with a survey by the *Sunday Times* which covered eighteen of the forty-three police-force areas in England and Wales, and revealed an overall drop in crime of around 5 per cent with 13 per cent fewer burglaries in London. However, burglaries in Avon and Somerset had risen by 6 per cent, violent crime was up by 17 per cent in Hampshire and over 25 per cent in Dyfed and Powys, while sexual crimes had increased by more than half in Lancashire and 32.5 per cent in Cumbria.

This is said to be evidence of an unprecedented crime wave in rural areas. In fact, it testifies only to the commentators' lack of historical perspective, to higher numbers of crimes being reported and to greater success in obtaining convictions. Of course robbers, drunks, drug addicts and bored youths exist, but so they always have. Agrarian unrest and riotous behaviour in country towns were far from unknown in the nineteenth century. The utopian model village with its quietly sleeping rude forefathers has been as much of a construct of the imagination as that other hamlet in which no Miss Marple could step beyond her hollyhock-guarded gate without finding the murdered corpse of a neighbour to investigate.

One of the main differences today is that increased security in urban properties has driven both professional and opportunist thieves to look for easier pickings out of town, and improved mobility means that not only the country closest to cities is at risk. Good roads mean that criminals can be 50 miles away from a burglary within the hour. If you live close to a motorway or major road which gives easy access to a city, you must be aware that commuting can be undertaken in either direction. Thus, while north Wales as a whole has a low crime rate, the A55 corridor is popular with thieves who can have a loaded pantechnicon in Liverpool within the hour. There are also certain crimes, including livestock rustling and the theft of garden ornaments, which are inevitably more common in country areas. Others, of course, including that constant infuriation of urban life, the pilfering of car radios, are much less prevalent. Smart cars, however, can be as much at risk as they are in town. Some of these considerations and contrasts are illuminated by the interview on the next page with a long-serving rural policeman.

# HOUSES

If better security in urban homes is driving criminals into the country, then country home-owners must beef up their own security. Alas, there are not that many places nowadays where doors can be left open without thought. Often it is as well to institute an evening locking-up routine; country properties, particularly if they are detached and surrounded by a garden, tend to be more vulnerable to burglars than terraced town houses, and even if

# Interview with Inspector Andy Howard

*COUNTRY LIFE*, 9 JULY 1998

Bakewell's senior policeman, Inspector Andy Howard, is an incomer. He was born in Liverpool, but spent his childhood in Mozambique, Egypt and Iraq – his father was a civil engineer. Living in foreign parts has left its impression: 'It still makes my wife laugh. Whenever I pick up a pair of shoes, I always clack them together and turn them upside down to check for scorpions.'

He then lived in Wales and in Derby until he got married. He and his wife have lived in Monyash (so called because of its proliferation of ash trees), an idyllic Derbyshire village, for the past nineteen years and are an integral part of the community. 'I was told by an old farmer when I moved here that I would never be accepted – my kids would probably not be accepted but their kids probably would.' In his mid-forties, with a weatherbeaten complexion and greying hair, he is an enthusiastic participant in village life, including the annual well-dressing ceremony which requires a week to build a clay board decorated with petals.

The village has changed quicker than that old farmer could have imagined. Nearly 40 per cent of the village houses are now holiday properties, the post office has closed and pupils are drafted from other areas to support the school. Inspector Howard thinks the new variety of incomers will bring their own problems. 'I don't think they mix very well with country people. They tend not to get involved with things.'

We met in the slate-roofed, granite police station that has served as the centre of law and order since it was built by the fifth Duke of Rutland in 1844. The Granby Road Lock-up, as it was then known, had a keeper until 1856, when it became compulsory to create a police force in every county. Prior to the arrival of the police, the parish had a police constable, a voluntary but time-consuming post. He employed a mole-catcher for £6 a year and paid a reward for killing foxes. 'If a constable was caught killing a fox now, he would probably have

100 animal liberationists besieging his address,' Inspector Howard chuckles.

A heavy-duty, rust-coloured padlock lies in a glass case, one of the few relics on display that remind visitors of the station's past. The original lock from 1844 was used until 1994, when the station was refurbished. Now Inspector Howard's office would not look out of place in an episode of *The Bill*. Grey filing cabinets fill three corners, and a small office year planner decorates the wall. There is a map of Derbyshire delineating the police divisions and a photograph of Chatsworth. Inspector Howard is dressed in summer uniform of black trousers and white short-sleeved shirt. The only contradiction to his chirpy, genial manner are the nails on the ends of thick, stubby fingers, which have been bitten right down. It may be that all the new equipment has made him nervous.

He bemoans the loss of his wooden truncheon. 'We used them for all sorts of things: breaking windows, banging in nails. They were very practical.' Now all the officers in the Bakewell police station are equipped more like New York cops. As well as the new, extendable metal baton which officers are trained to use on 'green areas' (such as the fingers of someone who refuses to get out of their car by hanging on to the steering wheel) and not 'red areas' (such as the head), there are handcuffs, a radio, access to police helicopter and CS gas. Officers are trained to use the gas before using the baton.

We are left reeling with images of internecine strife through the streets of Bakewell: farmers running down walkers with muck-spreaders, and vengeful pensioners stuffing Bakewell tarts through each other's letter boxes. Not so. The 25,500 people under Inspector Howard's jurisdiction are law-abiding. The criminals who tax the skills of his 36-member police force (plus 10 special constables) have usually come from outside.

The Peak District is the second most visited National Park in the world (Mount Fuji is first), and the vast numbers of tourists, walkers and climbers create rich pickings for the unscrupulous thief. 'The tourists bring vehicles that are targets for the villains. Strangers going through villages aren't that unusual, so people don't report them so much. We have put a team of officers on to deter auto crime and it has dropped by 40 per cent each year for the past three years. It is a rural area and it snows often in winter, so there are a lot of 4 x 4s, and there is a team targeting them. The trouble is if a farmer buys one, he won't put a tracker on it. I can guarantee that people in Sheffield with Range Rovers will have put trackers on their cars.' Cars are not the only problem. One man was recently in custody for being a 'ringer' (stealing to order) in tractors. Again the snorting chuckle. 'We've all heard of ringers in Porsches and Lamborghinis, but it would only be in an area like this that you would get someone doing it in tractors.'

Traditional crime for rural areas appears to be on the decrease, but not because of a special undercover operation. 'We have a little bit of rustling, but not as much as there was. I think it might be something to do with BSE. Poaching is not such a problem either. You can buy a brace of pheasants for £2 so it's not worth poaching for such a small return. There are a lot less countrymen now anyway.'

The main change he has witnessed in his policing career is in the attitudes of the young. 'I tend to get more telephone calls than I've ever had from people saying their nine- or ten-year old is out of control and can they bring him in to the police station and let him look at a cell. I used to help at youth clubs but about two years ago I decided I've had enough of this. The kids are just so disobedient. It's probably because they're not frightened of the police any more. I think we've effectively shot ourselves in the foot. We've tried to make inroads into the community and show ourselves as approachable, but it's a catch-22 situation.'

One gets the sense that his comments would apply to many of the socially deprived areas that the twentieth century has wrought on parts of Britain but not, surely, in Bakewell? Here the police are regarded almost as mascots. 'A lot of tourists come here. They're extremely friendly. They look on it as being like the television programme Heartbeat, and we are part of the tourist attraction. I have about five photographs taken of me every day. Even the locals would take it as a snub if you didn't say hello to them.'

As we leave to go there is no sign of the extendable baton and the CS gas, but when we get to the door Inspector Howard raises his arm. 'That's where you'll get the best Bakewell tarts in town,' he says, pointing to a discreet shop front before returning to the task of policing one of Britain's most rural, but also most visited, areas.

your house or cottage is quite small it may take longer to check all the doors and windows and draw the curtains.

*Secure by Design*, a pamphlet published by the Home Office, is a useful aid to security although it is aimed more at architects and planners than home-owners. The Hertfordshire Constabulary publish a practical booklet, *As Safe as Houses*, and similar booklets are available from other forces. They advise on basic security measures, such as window bolts, locks, security lights and thorny shrubs. A gravel drive – and gravel below area windows – will enable you to hear intruders. A dog is the best deterrent, but guinea fowl and geese are wonderfully noisy allies.

All this is general advice, but it is sometimes possible to arrange for a crime prevention officer (who may have a slightly different designation locally) to visit and advise you on your particular situation. He or she will indicate various commonsense precautions that you can take, usually working inwards from the perimeter of the property – whether it is an estate or a small garden – to the house itself, and ultimately to secure places within the building.

The officer may also offer practical advice on protecting animals and tack from thieves. Thin tack, for instance, such as reins, bridles and stirrup leathers, and heavily padded items should not be stamped as this will weaken them. Instead they should be marked with ultraviolet ink or a product such as SmartWater (see Directory, page 238). This is manufactured by the Forensic Science Service, a Home Office executive agency, and uses a concept similar to a DNA profile to mark objects in a way that is almost impossible to remove. Even a ballpoint pen will do. It is advisable to mark a horse with a proven commercial system such as freeze branding, which gives it a unique reference number. There are also accepted ways to record the physical descriptions of your animals.

Hair whorls are most important features for identifying a horse. There is always at least one on the forehead, and at least one on either side of the neck near the crest, either just behind the ears under the head collar, and/or along the neck. The colour, size, direction and positions of these whorls should be noted. Others may be on the breast, the windpipe towards the throat, on the flanks and, more rarely, on the legs.

# ART AND ANTIQUES

The theft of art and antiques from historic buildings – and indeed from buildings with no history at all – has been a serious problem in the United Kingdom for some time. A survey of 150 privately owned properties open to the public found that in a five-year period they had suffered 196 thefts or attempted thefts, in which 994 items to the value of £14,750,000 were taken. Only 7 per cent had been recovered.

The survey was undertaken by CoPat, the Council for the Prevention of Art Theft, which was founded in 1992 and brings together the police, insurance companies, the law, the antiques and fine art trade, the trade press and various crime prevention, risk assessment and heritage bodies. The organization's chairman, Mark Dalrymple, emphasizes that it is not in existence to protect only historic houses and high-value collections. 'We are equally concerned to protect the family heirlooms that are to be found in many homes in the country. These objects are not necessarily valuable in cash terms, but may be of great sentimental value to their owners.'

As irritating as being the victim of a burglary, and almost as distressing, is to find that you are the temporary beneficiary of one; that is to say, in receipt of stolen goods. Architectural recycling is only a little younger than architecture; many Renaissance palazzi were clad in marble stripped from the ruined palaces of imperial Rome, and fragments of dissolved monasteries were used in the construction of humbler buildings for miles around. The past century of demolition and development has seen not only legitimate cannibalizing of the remains of English country houses, and the growth of a flourishing trade in 'architectural antiques', but a parallel growth in architectural theft. Anyone who goes in search of a fire surround or grate, old tiles and bricks, a couple of columns or a balustrade, may unwittingly find themselves buying stolen property.

In 1995, after three years of consultation with colleagues and competitors, a group of dealers in architectural antiques, garden ornaments and salvaged building materials agreed to establish a code of conduct. They were already running an information service about stolen property under the name of Salvo (see Directory, page 236). This has now become a wide-ranging organization with nearly a hundred Salvo Code dealers, for the most part in Britain but also in France, Ireland, Canada and Australia.

Participants, and subscribers to Salvo's quarterly newsletter, receive theft alerts informing them about stolen items. The majority of these are garden ornaments and the rest are architectural features. If the item is in the area of a police force that subscribes to the Salvo theft alarm system, the service is free; otherwise the victim of the theft is charged £100.

Salvo recommends four simple measures to property owners, which may help to reduce the risk of theft:

1   Don't leave property unoccupied.
2   Photograph garden ornaments and any features in unoccupied buildings. Note any identifying damage or marks; also colour, materials, measurements and inscriptions.

3   Alert the police or a conservation officer if you see anyone suspicious in an unoccupied listed building or conservation area.

4   If an architectural or garden antique is stolen, first call the police, and then Salvo. Colour photocopy your photographs before handing them over to the police or Salvo.

Salvo's website has dealers' lists, a register of recommended craftsmen, details of auctions and much useful advice.

Codes of practice – in many trades and professions – are all very well, but a cynic might wonder whether they are not window dressing, lists of admirable intentions formulated when effective measures are in short supply.

In March 1999 CoPat came up with codes of due diligence. Like Salvo's code of conduct they are aimed at dealers and auctioneers offered goods by dubious vendors, but also emphasize the need to be aware of money-laundering operations and the wisdom of refusing to pay cash without full confidence in the vendor. At least as important are the crime and intelligence digests that CoPat circulates free of charge to over 1,500 heritage properties as well as to 1,000 named police officers in crime or intelligence bureaux around the country. These contain reports of people seen acting suspiciously, and details of thefts and attempted thefts of art and antiques not only from heritage properties but also from private houses.

Another welcome initiative is the object ID checklist (see Directory, page 237), which standardizes the description of fine art and antiques. The idea for this came from the Getty Information Institute, and it has been fully endorsed by CoPat. It enables any policeman – or indeed any buyer who suspects he is being offered stolen property – with no real knowledge of the subject to produce a sufficiently accurate description of what is in front of him for a victim of theft to recognize his property, or a dealer to recognize a stolen item.

# COMPUTERS

Computers and electronic communications equipment are obvious targets for burglars. On the whole theives are only interested in the latest equipment, which is why you may find that your computer and printer have been smashed rather than taken. If this should happen to you, make sure you overhaul your security thoroughly before installing replacements. The thieves will be back once they think that your insurance policy has supplied you with equipment more worthy of their attention.

# WATCH SCHEMES

People who are used to comparatively effective neighbourhood watch schemes in towns and cities may be frustrated by the lack of interest that some country people show in them. While village neighbours tend on occasion to notice more than one might wish, and the operations of the grapevine in truly rural communities defy scientific codification, the fruits may be hoarded rather than put to effective use. However, things are changing rapidly and increasing numbers of FarmWatch and country watch schemes are being established.

The country watch concept was the brainchild of PC Peter Hale of the Thames Valley force, who now not only advises and encourages other forces to set up schemes, but also acts as voluntary national coordinator. The first scheme went into operation in 1991 and since then it has been tried and tested on many occasions and never found wanting. Furthermore, not only has it been a major contributory factor in the reduction of crime in rural areas, it has had a positive effect on the quality of life of the people who live there.

A junior country watch project was launched in 1992. It organizes a week-long event each year and attracted well over 3,000 children aged between nine and eleven in its first seven

# You are being Watched

COUNTRY LIFE, SUE CORBETT, 9 SEPTEMBER 1999

Escalating rural crime has turned the farmers of Wearside and Teesdale into a suspicious bunch. Now when they see a high-sided van being driven round their area at the dead of night, they ask questions: does it contain a stolen quad bike, a rustled ewe or even 500 brace of poached grouse? From bitter experience, they know that the answer to at least one of these questions may very well be Yes. But, whatever the answer, they will get it in double-quick time via the FarmWatch operation they set up in 1990, which in 1995 became a cooperative venture with the Durham Constabulary.

Some 670 County Durham farmers, smallholders and other residents are members of the Wear and Tees FarmWatch, and forty or fifty of them turn out several nights a week to keep a watchful eye on their local patch. Parking their four-wheeled drives in the market square – or, if they can afford the diesel, scouting the country lanes round about – they watch all movements by road from late evening until the small hours, prime time for rural thefts.

The Durham Constabulary provide FarmWatch members with the registration numbers of all known criminal, or suspect, vehicles likely to be in their area. If the farmers see any of these vehicles, or any others they are unhappy about, they record their movements, and then call the police on their mobile telephones.

It works faster than that on the two or four nights a month that the police come out on a four-hour night patrol with the farmers. Plugging into the FarmWatch radio network, the police can respond to situations within minutes, as I discovered the night I went out in a marked police Land Rover with rural liaison officer PC Trevor Dawson. A big, jovial man, born and bred in the county and dedicated (if not addicted) to rural policing, he says: 'I cannot see how any vehicle can travel through Weardale or Teesdale at night and not be seen, with the amount of police and farmers' vehicles we turn out.'

And, within five minutes of our being tipped off by a FarmWatch member that a suspicious vehicle was on its way through Weardale, our flashing blue light had brought the high-sided hired van to a halt near the Blue Circle cement works at Westgate. Suspicions were heightened when PC Dawson found a calf travelling in the back of the van. The driver said he had just bought the calf from another local farmer, and that he was on his way home with it. Not a very likely story at 11.30pm, one might think. But many of the Durham dales smallholders work at other jobs during the day and do not find time until the evenings for their farming business. Police checks were made on the driver's story, and eventually other FarmWatch members radioed to vouch for both driver and van, who were at last allowed to continue on their way.

No Dales farmer or smallholder minds being stopped like this. The FarmWatch is his insurance against being burgled. 'Some thieves have told us they won't go into Weardale or Teesdale now because of the scheme,' PC Dawson says. The previous night, police on a FarmWatch patrol had arrested two men poaching in Teesdale. 'Poaching a couple of rabbits may seem petty,' PC Dawson says, 'but a lot of these people are also looking to see what farm equipment they can pilfer. When we check, more than 90 per cent of them are found to have criminal records.'

Watching and recording are all that the police ask their FarmWatch members to do. 'If our farmers record the same vehicles time and again in the vicinity of areas in which crimes have been committed, that can be useful evidence, leading to convictions,' PC Dawson says. 'We don't want them to get into any sort of confrontational situation. Rural thieves can be dangerous characters, and a car chase can always end in an accident.'

Wear and Tees FarmWatch was set up in 1990 by Peter Stubbs, its current chairman, who keeps cattle and poultry on a 70-acre small-holding at Kinninvie in Teesdale. Mr Stubbs today is a genial fellow with an engaging twinkle in his eye, but in 1990, like many other farmers, he was a desperate man. 'It had got to the stage,' he says, 'when there were farm thefts in Teesdale every week. If it wasn't sheep it was farm machinery. The police were doing a good job but there simply weren't enough of them, so my wife, Gladys, and I decided to organize a farm watch. If you're not seen to be helping yourselves, you're not going to get help from anybody else.'

The Wear and Tees FarmWatch which grew out of this Kinninvie group, now has its own radios, purchased with a grant of £10,000 from NFU Mutual, which insures about 80 per cent of the local farms. There is also a Crime Ring computer, bought with council grants and donations from local companies, which will automatically feed a telephone message to all 670 members.

Andy Naylor and Colin Thrower, two Environment Agency fisheries enforcement officers (formerly known as water bailiffs), were out on patrol the night I joined PC Dawson. Equipped with night-vision glasses and camera, they were keeping an eye on a nearby reservoir that had just been stocked with 7,000 rainbow trout. 'The fish are very saleable in the pubs, or door to door, and the naughty boys always know when a lot of them have been put in,' Mr Naylor says.

The villains adopt many guises. The day I met the Stubbses, they had been visited by so-called window cleaners, 'I guessed all they wanted to do was look into people's houses and then send someone else to raid them,' Mr Stubbs says. 'This is what happens. So our members tipped off the police, and it wasn't long before they had caught up with them, and warned them that, in this dale, FarmWatch members will always know exactly where they are – which should be enough to frighten them off.'

Mr Stubbs pays warm tribute to the police backing for FarmWatch: 'If the local superintendent and chief constable didn't sanction the expenditure and the manpower, we would get nowhere.'

years. Short scenarios are acted with the children to give them the awareness and ability to react to accidents, fires and other major incidents, as well as to report crimes and suspicious goings-on.

The first truly national country watch conference, in November 1998, attracted delegates from twenty-one forces, and it will not be long before the entire countryside is covered. A very important product of the scheme is that there is now much greater, and more efficient, cooperation between the forces in country areas than has traditionally been the case. This is also true of the neighbours who actually run the schemes. As PC Hale puts it, a scheme should not involve paperwork and meetings: 'In its simplest form, all it asks is that members talk to each other a bit more, become that little bit more security conscious, and contact the police as soon as they see or hear anything that causes them concern.'

Anyone wishing to know what is available and who to contact in their area, should get in touch with Peter Hale at Faringdon Police Station (see Directory, page 239). One of PC Hale's early disciples was PC Trevor Dawson in Durham (see page 95).

## GARDENS

The plundering of garden ornaments is as widespread as the theft of antiques and works of art – not just antique (and modern) statues from historic gardens, but urns and planters, cast-iron benches and other ornaments. Practical gardening equipment has also become extremely vulnerable, especially since ride-on mowers or tractors can represent an investment of some thousands of pounds. Not only farmers enthuse over quad bikes. They have become an accessory of choice among many country dwellers who have nothing to do with agriculture. As a result they are natural targets for thieves.

Sometimes insult is added to injury when the householder's own equipment is used to remove and transport statues or ornaments. In one such case thieves laid planks over a ha-ha – generally a line of defence that is not as old-fashioned as might be thought – and used a minitractor and trailer from the victim's garden to carry his ornaments across their makeshift bridge.

Plants are also targets, and it is not just a matter of green-fingered visitors sneaking cuttings. Considerable rarities are stolen by professionals and whole lawns and terraces are some-times removed. As long ago as 1992 there were reports of a whole back garden, including thirty trees and shrubs, the lawn and a stone bird bath being removed overnight at Blakeney in Norfolk; and of a daylight raid on a Sussex country house in which two men in wetsuits removed 300 lilies from a pond. Kew, Wisley, the Savill Gardens, the Ventnor Botanical Garden and many other important plant collections have all lost very valuable rarities.

As usual, this is not just a modern problem. In his *Encyclopaedia of Gardening*, published in 1827, the landscape designer Humphry Repton described the mantrap that was then in common use to catch thieves as 'a rat-trap on a large scale ... a barbarous contrivance though rendered absolutely necessary in the exposed gardens around great towns'. He preferred the version which, 'instead of breaking a leg by crushing and, consequently the worst of all compound fractures, simply breaks the leg and is therefore comparatively entitled to the appellation humane'.

In our differently humane times such deterrents are barred, but there is a whole technological industry to call on. Lights, alarms, cameras, bolts and sensors all have their place, but so do traditional methods, which may not be sophisticated but are none the less often effective.

◆ Put chains around the root ball of expensive trees and dig the chain into a trench to prevent uprooting.
◆ Place heavy weights such as bricks or rocks beneath the soil in large pots.
◆ Plant pretty but prickly shrubs such as berberis or pyracantha around ornaments.

◆ Loosely dug soil in flower beds around statues may produce a crop of footprints.

◆ Mark ornaments and valuable equipment. Insurers recommend Identidot (see Directory, page 238), which uses microdots, and SmartWater. And record the serial numbers on the equipment. It is not easy to identify the mower or chainsaw that used to be yours when you are in a police station or at a car boot sale.

◆ Keep a pair of binoculars near at hand.

◆ Lock up equipment securely.

◆ Cap hinges to prevent gates being lifted off them, and use case-hardened steel chains for padlocking.

◆ Keep photographic records.

# INSURANCE

The Jackson-Stops *Guide to the Insurance of Listed Buildings and Their Contents* (see Directory, page 229) – which is also of great use to owners of unlisted properties – makes the excellent point that where owners used to decide almost arbitrarily on the figure at which their houses should be covered, insurers are nowadays much more particular about establishing accurate rebuilding costs. Owners should not confuse market value with insurance valuation – or vice versa. The insurance valuation of a building relates to rebuilding only, and not to site value. Often the rebuilding costs of an old building will be more than the market value, while the replacement of a modern building may well be less.

The standard comprehensive cover includes: fire, lightning, explosion, aircraft, earthquake, storm, falling trees, burst pipes and escape of water, riot, malicious damage, impact, theft, flood, subsidence and perhaps accidental damage. Whether you live in a listed property or not, common sense may reduce this list, and thus the annual premium somewhat. An old house should have long settled, and so subsidence is likely only if its external circumstances have changed. For instance there may have been mining since it was built. This would be the only reason to insure against subsidence if you have a house that is solidly built on rock. Equally, flood is not usually a great danger on a hilltop but could be a risk if your property is close to a river. Fire, storm and burst pipes are the most constant perils.

So far as contents insurance is concerned, many people have lost touch with the true replacement value of their possessions. Others are underinsured because they have not thought about the cumulative value of what they have acquired over years. You may think this doesn't concern you but, as television programmes like *The Antiques Roadshow* have shown, many more people unknowingly own valuable works of art or antiques than might be supposed. Furthermore, it is not uncommon for an unpretentious three- or four-bedroom house to contain £30,000 worth of books.

If you suspect you have a treasure in your attic – or think you may have unearthed one in the cellar of your new country house – it is well worth getting it valued. Valuation is a matter of experience, and in many cases it is simplest to go to a recommended dealer or auctioneer. However, this begs the question of conflicting interests and even the highest reputations are not always proof against temptation. A few years ago, in London criminal circles, the head of the valuations department of one auction house was generally referred to as 'Uncle So-and-so'. Some people feel safer using an impartial valuation company and details of three are included in the Directory (page 240).

All too many owners of antiques or other valuable objects still have them insured as part of their run-of-the-mill contents policies. These are inflexible, and may have unrealistic single-article limits, such as 5 per cent of the sum insured. High net worth insurance is often the best bet if you have an object that you value particularly, whether it be for monetary or sentimental reasons. Several insurance groups offer dedicated fine arts covers or high net worth contracts (see Directory, page 239). Such a specialized cover can usually be run alongside a smaller household policy, with the two costing less than a conventional contents quotation. Here I speak from personal experience, and I enjoy the further advantage that, having done my research properly, I can bin all those impertinently winsome letters from banks, building societies and even brokers, who claim that they can undercut my present premiums. If you do not wish to insure an item such as a family heirloom fully, it is possible to part-insure it. You then take the uninsured part of the risk on yourself.

So far as accidental damage is concerned, the major difference between a standard policy and a specialist one is depreciation. The insurer can indemnify an owner for the cost of restoration and the consequential fall in value. This would not be covered by a household contents policy. Gradual deterioration caused by heat, light, wear and tear is a universal exclusion, but the insurance company can offer informed advice on how to prevent, or lessen, it. During client visits advice will be offered not only on security measures, but also on such matters as the effects of central heating and sunlight on furniture, watercolours and textiles, or damp and water on wood and other materials.

As yet few companies operate policies specifically for electronic equipment – one that does is listed in the Directory (page 240) – but it cannot be long before this becomes standard insurance practice. Until then, it would be wise to shop around – and always back up your work and keep secure copies of your records.

# CHAPTER SIX

# WORKING OR RUNNING A BUSINESS FROM HOME

It should be no surprise to learn that self-employment is proportionately much higher in rural areas than elsewhere. Working for yourself is a privilege anywhere, and it can be even more of a pleasure in the country. Statistics, in so far as they have a meaning, support its popularity. In the rural development areas of Devon, North Yorkshire and East Sussex self-employment stands at 26 per cent, with Cornwall, Hereford and Worcester following at 25 per cent. Combining a move with working from home, or setting up a business in the new property, is immensely tempting and can produce exciting challenges.

If you have never been self-employed before, you will find that there is rather more to it than you might have imagined. In particular, there is the problem of loneliness. This is, of course, something that affects anyone who works from home even if they are based in a town or city, but you are likely to be even more solitary in the country. You must be sure that you enjoy your own company and, ideally, that there are ways in which you can see fellow professionals, or at least stimulating and interested friends, on a regular basis in order to exchange ideas and maintain a sense of proportion. Given the increase in self-employment in country areas, it should be possible to set up routines and networks with like-minded people, so that you have a chance to talk through problems and, as importantly, discuss triumphs. Naturally, nowadays the most immediate channel of help is the Internet.

For me, working from home is the only way to work – although I do enjoy an occasional few hours in an office just to remind me how lucky I am. I have been a home-based freelance for the best part of thirty years, and I cannot really understand how other people can be happiest in a structured office environment. However, I do – just – remember the panic of my first days on my own. I suppose there always will be some element of this, as every new venture is a gamble, but nowadays there is so much more help and support than when I first started to work from home, when the 'office' consisted solely of a telephone and a typewriter. Certainly, the rapid advances in telecommunications and computer technology obviously make self-employment a practical option for more and more people – and this applies particularly to anyone working in the country.

Even if you are confident that working alone holds no terrors for you, it is not just a question of setting up a computer, a potter's wheel, or whatever, and winging away. Office discipline is essential. It may be necessary to establish a practical demarcation line between working and family times. And you must make it absolutely plain to all friendly neighbours that dropping in is very unwelcome except at lunchtime, or after the hour that you shut up shop. The smaller the community you settle in, the greater the possibility that you could be roped in for charitable and social work, which can be very satisfying but could take up a great deal of your supposedly paid day.

This was made very clear to me, during a telephone conversation at 10.30 one midweek morning, by a friend who has recently moved to Gloucestershire and works from her home there. My admiration for her iron self-discipline would have been greater had she not concluded: 'Must stop now. I have promised to help out for a couple of hours with writing the parish magazine'. Her small village has a thirteenth-century church and a school hall, for which funds must be raised. Another friend, also self-employed, found herself made chairman of the primary school governors within two years of arriving in a Berkshire village.

Self-sufficiency is another important aspect of working in the country. Sir Roy Strong, writer, garden designer and former director of the Victoria and Albert Museum, moved to Herefordshire about thirty years ago with his wife, the theatre designer Julia Trevelyan Oman. They rapidly learned the importance of looking ahead. 'Always buy in bulk,' he says, 'whether it's stationery or iron rations.' He and his wife went one step further and set up an alternative source of electricity: 'We still get power cuts,' he says, 'which would be fatal to any writing, but our own generator can have us up and running again in fifteen minutes.'

Sir Roy also points out, delicately, that if two or more people are working from the same home tact as well as discipline is needed to balance the pleasure of company with the possibility of distraction.

It is also sensible to make sure that the property you want to buy is in the right place for the kind of work you will be doing. For example, will you be able to communicate quickly and easily with clients? As yet not everywhere has the efficient communications promised by IT. In particular, at present ISDN only operates reliably if you are close to an exchange, although properties along the lines of motorways are better served. This will not apply for much longer, but could be a disadvantage in the short term.

A possible solution to this problem, and an alternative to the solitariness of working at home, is provided by the rapidly increasing numbers of rural office centres. These may be in market towns, on small industrial estates or, often the most pleasant, in recycled estate buildings. A well-built stable yard can house several businesses, whether one-person or with several employees. All sorts of services, from cleaning and security to stationery buying, post services and bookkeeping, can be shared or coordinated, and there is also the stimulus of working with like-minded people.

Ideally, the office should be within fifteen minutes drive of your property if the advantages of self-employment are not to be dissipated by excessive school runs, childhood illnesses, dashes to town and crisis drives of all sorts. And it is a good idea to have technical back-up at home so that it is possible to work there if necessary.

An office centre has the additional advantage that there will be someone to take messages for you when you are away. If you do work from your home, never leave an 'I'm on holiday' message – an invitation to burglars – on your answerphone. Have messages diverted and, if possible, arrange for someone to respond to them within twenty-four hours during any absence. This will help to keep your clients happy. Similarly, have mail and parcels delivered to a neighbour when you are away.

## SMALL BUSINESSES

Running a business that requires employees is naturally more complex than working by yourself, and some questions need to be answered before you make your move to the country. Is the property really right? Not everywhere is suited to doubling as a home and an office. Might there be transport difficulties for employees, clients or suppliers? Are you aware of the health and safety regulations? The more people you employ, the more planning regulations will materialize.

Choose your working area as carefully as your premises and family circumstances allow. Noise levels can be a two-way problem, depending on your equipment and your family's musical tastes. Equally, you may need to separate business and family visitors. Check if you need planning permission to put up a business sign.

When equipping an office concentrate on what you must have, rather than what it would be nice to have. Make sure you have enough space and comfortable equipment for anyone who may be working with you. Consider your communications needs carefully, and find out about the best equipment offers and deals. Set up computer back-up programmes as a precaution against fire, power failures, burglary or – perish the thought – your own incompetence. Keep secure copies of vital records and make sure that all computers and communications equipment are properly insured.

It may very well take some time to find employees with the particular combination of skills and availability that you require – not everyone in the country is anxious to work full- or part-time for the home-based businesses of incomers – and the early stages may be particularly testing as you face the challenge of getting your business up and running before you have had time to develop the social network that will find you the best help.

A top London public relations practitioner who relocated life and business to an East Anglian manor house, did find fully trained local help. Unfortunately, the manor's roof needed replacing and before long the perfect office assistant had run off with the ideal roofer. This left the employer not just without help, but with no certainty as to the re-roofing. Instead there were all too regular interruptions by the roofer's irate wife who, alas, could not even type, much less compose a press release. If you have settled within the gravitational pull of a prosperous town, especially one with good transport connections, you may find it more difficult still to recruit suitable employees as many people will prefer to seek work in the town itself.

Because of the distances they may have to travel, employees in the country tend to start and finish work earlier, especially in winter. This is only one of the ways in which it may be necessary to manage time differently: telecommunications may take seconds, but physical things, such as ordering motorbike couriers, or driving vital mail to the nearest post office, can take far longer. If you need a courier you may have to order him the day before.

However, there are time-saving services that are not available in towns. If your business is in the real countryside, whether at home or in an office centre, it is well worth seeing if you can arrange for your postman to pick up mail at the same times as he delivers it. This used to be a standard service for the estate offices of large country houses, and is one that new businesses should insist on preserving or reviving. Indeed, everyone must be prepared to fight to keep the postman. Milkmen, too, may deliver more than just the milk.

Meetings will be more complicated to organize because allowances must be made for travelling times, and maintaining contacts will take more work. You won't be able to drop into a client's office to see if there is any work, and casual meetings in the street or pub will be a thing of the past.

The profit a dear friend made when she sold her London flat and bought the country cottage of her dreams was big enough to give her a false sense of security. She let her business coast and spent a year getting the cottage and garden right, with the result that she never really won back her old London clients when she was ready to work for them again – and rather urgently needed them. If you run any kind of established service it is essential to reassure your existing metropolitan or international clients that your change of address will involve no inconvenience to them, either at the time of moving or later.

Unless your property is really remote, most of the small businesses you need in order to run your own will be within reach in the local town. However, printers and other companies whose services may be vital to you are less likely than their urban counterparts to provide quality and competitive rates, if only because they will enjoy a virtual monopoly in the area. And remember to fix early closings and half days firmly in your mind.

# BACK-UP

If you are setting up a small business, it is vital to consult a solicitor, an accountant and a bank manager on the legal, tax and financial implications of your proposed business plan. Check that you and your buildings will be suitably insured. Most high street banks offer useful start-up packs, which can take some of the complacency or panic (depending on your nature) out of the initial stages. For instance, the NatWest *Start-up Guide* takes you gently from 'thinking about it' to 'up and running'. Three-quarters of the way through there is a page of sixty-seven questions, starting with 'Do I really want to go into business?' and ending with 'Am I determined to go ahead?'. Banks also offer legal advice, guides for employers and information for sole traders and partnerships.

If you are a one-man (or woman) business you will not require such detailed information, but you will need the help of a bank for banking wisdom, an accountant for the books and a solicitor for the legal side.

Whether you will be running a small business or working alone, an aspect that needs to be thought through with your bank at the outset is your likely cash flow. Many small businesses will bring in little during the early phases, especially if there are considerable setting-up costs and loans to be serviced, while others bring in the profits intermittently, rather than regularly as an accountant would wish.

However small your business, there is no need to feel that you are alone. Together with the other organizations listed in the Directory (see page 241), there are a number of bodies on the Internet devoted specifically to the needs of the self-employed. A first call might be to OwnBase, which has been providing back-up for people working from home, whether as an employer or alone since 1986. The network is available to members not only to advertise themselves and their products or services, but to pick the brains of fellow members and benefit from their experience. There is a quarterly newsletter, as well as a directory of members and a series of information sheets on home working.

The OwnBase philosophy is encouraging: it is 'about helping people to achieve a balance amongst all the things they care about, while dealing well with the varied joys and the many practicalities of being home based.'

Two other very useful web sites are those of Home Run (*Better Business*), which is closely involved with the web-site designer Siserone; and Home Business Alliance, which has been in operation since 1993 and gives home businesses a voice commensurate with their numbers. *Better Business* is the United Kingdom's leading subscription-only magazine for the self-employed and offers practical, down-to-earth help, as well as contacts, to microbusinesses and freelancers. Siserone offers expertise in designing websites for new small businesses. The Home Business Alliance is primarily angled at small businesses and enables them to present a united front to officialdom, which tends to respect the power of numbers. It also provides legal and financial advice at little or no cost and organizes useful discounts on such necessities as printing, advertising and office furniture, and a free newsletter is published ten times a year. Details of all three web sites are in the Directory (page 241).

Among other checklists, The Institute of Management (see Directory, page 242) publishes *Running a Small Business from Home*. This covers the law, insurance, tax, the office and its equipment, security and neighbours' rights among other vital topics and lists five advantages and three disadvantages of working from home. The former are: cost savings as a result of eliminating the overheads of separate premises; low start-up costs and no rent; time saved by cutting out commuting; tax relief (perhaps); flexibility of working hours. The disadvantages are: loss of part of your home; interruptions and distractions by family, friends and yourself; possible friction with neighbours if you have frequent deliveries, noisy machinery or so many visitors that they become intrusive. Success, says the institute, depends on self-motivation and on sound planning and preparation.

Much of the advice offered by these organizations is common sense, and that is as it should be.

# BIGGER BUSINESSES

Of course, it is not only small businessmen and women who set up in the country, and the owners and managers of large concerns that are established from scratch or relocated, may face an entirely different set of circumstances. Generally speaking, new companies are likely to be welcomed with open arms, as they bring employment and prosperity with them. If you are moving to the country because the company you work for has relocated you will already have a circle of friends among your colleagues, and it will be easy to make contacts among local recruits. This can be an enriching experience for all, not least those people who are lucky enough to have been moved at the company's expense, and whose houses have been found for them.

However, in an imperfect world not every relocation will go that smoothly. Just as a proposed bypass will often place residents and outsiders, especially ecologists, in violently opposed camps, so the setting up or development of a business may have unfortunate repercussions for both incomers and older residents. Currently there are disputes over Vodaphone's proposed headquarters at Newbury (still catching its breath after the bypass fight), the Wellcome Trust's genetics complex in Cambridgeshire, which has recently been given a planning thumbs down, and many more or less serious disputes about out-of-town superstores and similar developments. Very often almost everybody involved has at least some right on their side, and for the good of all it is as well to seek a compromise before feuds are established for the next generation to live with.

# CHAPTER SEVEN

# GARDENS
# AND FARMLAND

Tony Venison, former gardening editor and now gardens
consultant to *Country Life*, advises any potential buyer of
a house with an established garden to ask themselves one
question before they plunge: do you like what is actually there?

A couple of years ago one of my brothers-in-law, Julian Rowse,
moved out of London so that his young family might be brought
up in the countryside. His own upbringing had been divided
between town and country, but his independent adult life had been
spent in Fulham with a tiny backyard. He wanted a large house,
and the area had to be convenient for his work in Ascot. This essentially limited him to the outermost suburban belt in Hampshire,
and there he did indeed find a suitable house. However, it came
with 8 acres of gardens and woodland, and a sizeable pond. The
gardens were not just a random happenstance of flower beds and
lawns, but had been professionally laid out by Jane Fearnley-
Whittingstall, gold-medal winner at the Chelsea Flower Show.

Hitherto Julian's style had been more Gucci than green welly,
and his first reaction was that he would have to grass over almost
everything. After all, he believed, for economy and ease of maintenance grass and trees are best. However, this would have been

to desecrate a work of art, rather as if one were to paint over a series of murals inside a house because they didn't suit a current fashion for minimalism. While it might have been the right house, for a time it seemed as though this had been the wrong property for him to have bought.

In any case, vast swathes of empty grass are not usually the most pleasing surroundings for a house, just as a disused walled garden that has been grassed over is generally a sad sight. If you are tempted to do such a thing to a walled garden, remember that it could be let commercially – it will look a great deal better, and perhaps provide you with payments in kind in addition to income.

Luckily the challenge of what was there soon sparked Julian's interest, and he did not grass over the beds. He had realized the wisdom of another of Tony Venison's maxims: simplification is rarely simple. Any major alterations to an established layout can be expensive, and the subsequent maintenance of even basic shapes requires a lot of labour. However, mere size need not be daunting as the maintenance of a carefully designed half-acre may actually require more work than a larger area.

Rather than quote Tony Venison in snippets and snatches, and since I could not possibly better the advice he provided for the 1989 *Country Life* and Knight Frank guide to *Buying a Country House*, I am pleased that he has agreed to let me print the revised version on the next page. It might, however, be worth expanding on one point that he touches on in passing, especially since it allows me to air a theory of my own which has yet to be tested scientifically but which, if I cannot posit it in my own book, probably never will be.

The 'reasonably mild microclimate' of Lionel Fortescue's garden at Buckland Monachorum in Devon, which Tony mentions on page 119, is not a solitary phenomenon. It may not be possible to say why such sites were originally chosen, but many monastic and ecclesiastical foundations seem to have climates that are on average several degrees warmer than the areas that surround them. It is partly because the lie of the land gives shelter,

# What about the Garden?

TONY VENISON; *BUYING A COUNTRY HOUSE* (1989)

Relatively few home-purchasers put their special garden requirements before the choice of a house when searching for a suitable property. Normally they have clear-cut notions of the type of house that is wanted. It is rather less usual for them to stipulate to agents that they are looking for a walled kitchen garden, a range of greenhouses or a grotto, or that the layout should have been carried out to designs by Thomas Mawson, Percy Cane, Lanning Roper, or some other renowned landscaper.

But if a prospectus mentions that the garden is the work of a notable designer, or that it has belonged to a well-known gardener, such a cachet may swing the balance. Shortcomings in the house may then be overlooked. A garden by a distinguished designer, or planted by a celebrated gardener, can generally be assumed to be a place possessing character. As with houses and period furniture, gardens that rise above the commonplace are in demand and command a premium.

The size of a garden and its outliers frequently affects the choice of a property. Privacy and isolation are often expressed criteria, and may necessitate the acquisition of a large garden area to enclose and protect the house against the clamour, overcrowding, pollution and inquisitiveness of the outside world.

A garden's setting and the views seen from it should be taken into account. There may be unsightly farm buildings or a housing development which would require screening off. An idyllic pastoral scene or quiet river valley can be rapidly ruined by an adverse planning decision resulting in a new road, building activity or quarrying. Enquiries to local authorities, road transport departments, river authorities, the Council for the Protection of Rural Engand – and especially among local people – help to bring any actual proposals and hints of future proposals to light.

During the late 1940s and the 1950s with owners bedevilled by acute shortages of labour and materials, crippling taxation and an unpromising future, large gardens became a burden. Many which fell into ruin then, or were considerably reduced in size, are being restored and expanded today.

Opportunities to acquire rundown, important historic or plantsmen's gardens continue to occur. Although the nation's most highly valued gardens are now officially listed under the auspices of English Heritage, and in most areas further lists are being compiled, few statutory restraints control the alteration or even destruction of these gardens. An owner is still very largely free to pursue his own policies. A tree, maybe capable of growing 80 feet high, which will dominate the landscape when fully grown, can be planted almost anywhere, whereas the siting of a flagpole is subject to official planning consent.

However, the cutting down or lopping of a tree necessitates permission being sought if that tree is the subject of a tree preservation order, or if it is within a local authority's conservation area. Before a property is acquired, an enquiry into the existence of such orders and restrictions should be made to the local authority. In cities it is not unusual for a tree, with its roots reaching down into the house foundations and drainage pipes, and its branches darkening the rooms, to be protected in this manner. Only fruit trees and trees on Crown property are exempt from these orders.

A prospective purchaser who wishes to learn something of a garden's history might first turn to a suitable second-hand bookshop or the Internet in hopes of tracking down Ray Desmond's *Bibliography of British Gardens*. Originally published in 1984, this lists published articles concerning 5,500 gardens in Britain. Enquiries made to the relevant county archives department or local library or museum may also be fruitful. Initial correspondence should be addressed to the Membership Secretary, 5 The Knoll, Hereford HR1 1RU.

When viewing a garden it is highly advisable to ascertain whether any full-time or part-time help is employed in it and, if so, whether accommodation is provided for them. What this assistance involves in financial terms should be understood, including the employer's national insurance and superannuation contributions, especially since garden-ers' salaries vary not only in different areas of the country, but also as to the value put on the individual.

The sale of a property has been known to hinge upon whether a gardener would be willing to stay on and work for the prospective new owners. Today, with trained students leaving horticultural colleges and centres such as the National Trust for Scotland's School of Gardening at Threave, perhaps such a proviso merits less consideration. On the other hand, conscientious, experienced gardeners who can manage a garden and develop or maintain character are in considerable demand. Many garden owners also work hard at their own gardens. So a garden kept without paid assistance cannot be assumed to be labour-saving even if the vendor casually remarks that, 'It really is not any trouble'.

While gardens of 2 to 4 acres are in demand, and larger ones are also snapped up by enthusiastic buyers, sales of properties with smaller gardens continue unabated. As Gertrude Jekyll wrote: 'The size of a garden has little to do with its merit.' Reginald Farrer – gardener, plant hunter and explorer – went further in commenting: 'A little garden, the littler the better, is your richest chance of happiness and success.'

Logically, purchasers might be expected to fall into two categories: those prepared or even anxious to undertake the restoration or making of a garden, and those for whom an established well-maintained garden, which will require no alterations, is vital. But preconceived ideas are not invariably the controlling factors. Mrs Basil Barlow has described in *The New Englishwoman's Garden* (1987) how she and her husband first viewed Stinchcombe, near Dursley in Gloucestershire, while it lay shrouded in thick autumn fog. When this lifted, revealing the landscape, and sunlight lit the russet tints of the trees, 'Then and there we decided that this was where we wanted to live,' she recalls. Not until after their decision did they discover that they were the purchasers of a somewhat derelict 15 acre garden with a folly and three lakes.

At Stinchcombe the outcome was a happy one; the vision and professional gardening expertise of Lanning Roper, Peter Coats and

Fred Whitsey were called upon. Although some of the finest gardens in Britain today, including Sissinghurst, Hidcote and Kiftsgate, were the creations of their owners, these owners were so committed to, and knowledgeable about, gardening that to term them amateurs is a misnomer. An intending purchaser of a property could well feel justified in calling in a reliable garden design consultant, at least to suggest an outline plan and advise on the basic running costs.

To anyone unaccustomed to gardening, these costs can seem surprisingly high. The late Lanning Roper complained bitterly that at one property about which he was consulted, the expenditure on new curtains for the house exceeded the total budget allotted for laying out the entire garden of several acres. John Sales, the former chief gardens adviser to the National Trust, estimates tree planting in terms of at least £100 per tree. This includes not only soil and site preparation, the cost of the tree (£30 or so for a good standard), but also its stake and ties, stem-guard against rabbits, and initial maintenance. For a site requiring drainage and planting with rare species and special varieties or with extra-heavy standards or semi-mature trees, the sums involved are much greater.

Would-be purchasers, and vendors too, often fail to realize the asset-value of existing garden features. One greenhouse in good structural condition, fitted with a modern, efficient heating system and perhaps also an automatic watering system and a mist propagator, can represent several thousand pounds. It was only after a 1930s property went on the market in Essex a few years ago at £250,000 that the owner consulted Sotheby's, whose experts put an estimated value of more than £80,000 on its lead garden ornaments, which had not been taken into account by the estate agents.

The acquisition of a mature garden is equivalent to buying time, or even sometimes results stemming from the work of several lifetimes. A handsome tulip tree (*Liriodendron tulipifera*) takes, on average, twenty years to attain a height of 20 feet, and sixty years to gain its maximum of 90 feet. Similarly, a cedar of Lebanon (*Cedrus lebanii*) can only be expected to be 14 feet tall when fifteen years old, about 40 feet when forty-three years old, and not until it has been growing freely for 125 years will it begin to reach its full majestic stature.

Today a 6–8-foot tall decorative holly in a container in a nursery is priced upwards of £150. But view an avenue of these hollies, planted out 50–100 years ago, and now grown at least three times as tall, clipped, and providing evocative period character to a Victorian or Edwardian house. What is the value of these hollies now, in all the glory that their original owner may not have lived sufficiently long to see?

Trees can provide traps for the unwary. Clothed in full leaf, they can be the glory of a garden. Where they abound, however, a visit by an accredited tree expert may avert the pitfall of purchasing a property where a high proportion of trees are diseased or approaching old age, near to death, or dangerous, or in need of tree surgery, bracing, thinning out, or felling. The Arboricultural Association maintains a list of its members, throughout Britain, professionally qualified to undertake such examinations. The address is Ampfield House, Ampfield, near Romsey, Hampshire SO51 9PA.

Garden enthusiasts will be quick to enquire about the nature of a garden's soil. For Mr Lionel Fortescue, who created the now famous garden at Buckland Monachorum in Devon, an acid soil in which to cherish rhododendrons, camellias, magnolias and suchlike choice lime-haters was essential. So, too, the reasonably mild microclimate. Few purchasers, whether gardeners or not, relish a frost pocket, likeliest to occur in a valley or hollow rather than on a hillside where frosts can flow harmlessly away downhill, if unobstructed.

An excess of shade can also pose problems, particularly on enclosed, north-facing sites. Unwelcome prevailing winds should be screened off by shelterbelts, walls or fences, either existing or taken into account as part of the property's future developments. Taking note of other gardens in the vicinity and visiting those open to the public can be especially rewarding in revealing whether relatively tender plants prosper, the sturdiness and nature of the prevailing vegetation, and whether it appears to be waterlogged or starved. It is worth risking a rebuff – rarely forthcoming – by telephoning and seeking information from owners of gardens in the vicinity and listed in the 'Yellow Book', *Gardens of England and Wales*, published annually by The National Gardens Scheme, Hatchlands Park, East Clandon, Guildford, Surrey GU4 7RT.

Sir Frederick Ashton would probably have asserted that he chose his Suffolk home at Chandos Lodge, Eye, 'in spite of the garden' which he began to make by 'sitting and looking and getting into a kind of state'. And Mr and Mrs Martin Lane Fox stressed that they had 'accepted the challenge of an unsuitable house and garden' before they began to make their delightful garden at Hazelby House in Berkshire. So, when all practical, financial historical and aesthetic considerations have been pondered, the immensely personal decision to 'take on' a garden often depends upon an individual's innermost feelings impossible to quantify or explain. It must 'feel right.'

but I suspect that an instinctive skill, akin to dowsing, may also have been employed. No doubt this is a contributory factor to the tranquillity of such places, as it certainly is to their fecundity.

I first became aware of the possibility that more than the odour of sanctity was involved some years ago when I visited the former Augustinian Leez Priory in Essex. So irenic a spot is it that a sixteenth-century owner was told that he 'had need make sure of heaven, or else when you die you'll be a great loser'; and a hundred years later the great Earl of Cork, brother-in-law of another owner, christened it 'delicious Leez'. Today the plants at Leez still are markedly ahead of those in neighbouring gardens.

# WATER AND WORKS

One point that Tony does not touch upon is the passionate desire of many of us to create a pond, if not a small lake, where there was none before. A recent report in *The Times* underscored the most basic potential hazard: 'We started to dig in a corner of the field which had natural banks on either side. But soon after we started, someone came running up the lane and said "Stop! You've hit a high-pressure water mains." It wasn't listed on our deeds.'

It is easy to be wise after the event, but that family might have been sensible to employ a dowser to walk over the site. Deeds and surveys are not always exhaustive, and it may be that a forgotten drain or watercourse does indeed lurk beneath a lawn or field. I retain an open-to-favourable mind about dowsers. I have met several who seemed to produce results – one during an unusually dry summer when it really mattered – and my one personal experiment was more successful than unsuccessful.

Positioning is vital to the successful establishment of even the most modest pond. If it is to be small and purely ornamental, it should not be under a tree that will shed leaves into it, although an exception might be made for a miniature willow if you are aiming at an Oriental effect. However, if you are thinking of establishing a comparatively large pond, leaves may actually be useful, since they will help to build up a natural base. Although it is tempting, avoid putting in so many lilies that they cover most of the water. Roughly one-third of a small pond's surface should be covered, because too much sunlight breeds algae and turns the water green, but too many lily pads and you will not be able to enjoy your fish. Also, the more lilies in your pond, the more rotting material will have to be cleared.

If you do decide on a pond larger than town garden size, you may need to do more than just your homework first. If you are intending to use part of a field or paddock, and to surround the water with a new area of garden, you may well have to get planning permission for change of use from agricultural land. In addition, will your chosen site need levelling or even draining? What kind of soil do you have? Clay, for instance, drains poorly and you may need to design some sort of overflow system. On the other hand, if the water table is low you are likely to need some sort of rubber lining. I have known people who used layers of black plastic bags. I have also learned that it was unwise to ask about some of the resulting ponds a year or two later, since the water had seeped away.

Books can be a great help – and *Ponds and Water Gardens* by Bill Heritage (see Directory, page 245), originally published in 1981, is still one of the best – but their wisdom may be irrelevant to your conditions. If you want to create anything more than a small decorative pond the only sure way to do so is to put yourself in the hands of an experienced enthusiast with a proven local track record. Similarly, if you want to install a swimming pool (or build a tennis court) you will need to go to an expert.

# WILDLIFE AND DEATH

'Feather-footed through the plashy fen passes the questing vole...' according to Evelyn Waugh's great fictional newspaper naturalist William Boot, but the only voles most people see are the pathetic little eviscerated corpses deposited on the kitchen floor by questing cats. Death and killing seem more natural in the country than in towns and cities. Farm cats do more than play with birds and mice; they earn their keep. Terriers kill rabbits, including those suffering from myxomatosis, and a good thing too; with luck and encouragement they will also keep down the rat population. An explosive population of healthy rabbits in a warren may require more professional skills. In Derbyshire you would be lucky indeed if you could secure the services of a team widely referred to as 'poachers by appointment to the Duchess'.

Sentimentality can be more akin to cruelty than kindness, and even if you have no sympathy for blood sports, you may find that you have to steel yourself to twist the neck of a wounded bird cleanly. If you keep chickens you may also find that you are keeping foxes – and that they are not the amiable gourmets of sophisticated urban dustbins. Deer are decorative, but will not necessarily accord well with your trees and shrubs. It is up to you to decide how to reconcile the two.

However small your garden, it may harbour a wasps' nest that has to be destroyed; or your immaculate patch of lawn may one morning be mountainous with mole hills. Both problems will need professional, or at any rate experienced, attention, and the professors charge vastly different rates according to the prosperity of the area, and, perhaps, the local standing of the customer.

# VEGETABLE PATCHES

Killing is also a fact of life if you wish to cultivate produce for your table. Slugs and bugs of all sorts become your enemies, but this will not necessarily mean resorting to chemical warfare. The Henry Doubleday Research Association (see Directory, page 243) is the leader in the organic field – the Prince of Wales is its patron – and publishes a series of fact sheets on controlling pests, from ants and aphids to vine weevils, as well as further fact sheets and leaflets on disease and weed control and general gardening topics. A thoroughly practical organic organization, the HDRA also publishes step-by-step guides to organic gardening and an admirable list of books. Its gardens in Coventry contain demonstration plots that illustrate the advice contained in its publications.

I always think that one of the incidental pleasures in gardening is the felicity of the names of so many gardeners and gardening writers. Several of the HDRA's books, including *Pests, How to Control them on Fruit and Vegetables*, and *All about Compost* are written by Pauline Pears and Charlotte Green.

There are several good reasons for cultivating a vegetable patch, and economy is not generally one of them. Enjoyment of the work and the satisfaction of serving home-grown produce are their own rewards, while knowing that vegetables are as organic as the gardener wishes them to be is a vital bonus for many.

If you want to grow vegetables on a large scale you might try to find a property with a walled garden, large or small, and then make sure you have both the financial and physical resources for what will virtually be a business. However, most people are looking for a hobby, rather than a full-time occupation, even though it may become more of a consuming interest than they expect.

There are several very basic rules for choosing a suitable area for a small vegetable patch. It is important that it is not shaded by trees, as most vegetables – spinach is perhaps an exception – like sunlight. It should also be fairly sheltered from wind, and must not be a frost pocket. Apart from such permanent features as beds of asparagus (which takes several years to establish) and seakale, most people hope to grow embellishments for their table: salad crops and, increasingly as the British climate grows warmer, tomatoes and even peppers, which once upon a time used to be grown only in greenhouses.

If you are planning rather more than just a small vegetable plot, there are two approaches. The traditional layout is the 'trooping of the colour': serried ranks organized vegetable by vegetable in large beds. Currently fashionable is the potager style, with everything in small beds within a network of criss-crossing paths.

As ever, the Royal Horticultural Society (see Directory, page 244), can tell you anything you might need to know, and very much more, but there are two organizations of particular interest to home cultivators. The National Vegetable Society (see Directory, page 243) is principally concerned with exhibiting, but is also a source of practical information.

# AGRICULTURE

Beyond the boundaries of your own cultivated area, whether large or small, there may well be a wider world of agriculture, and it might be as well to know something about it. You may find that you feel proud to be part of a farming community that has supported generations and still relies on local and family labour. It is worth knowing where your food comes from and how it is grown, because you will then be able to defend what you believe the countryside stands for, in the real knowledge of what makes it tick.

Farming, as we all know, is in crisis. Farmers tell us so and request our sympathy, but they find themselves on the horns of a herd of dilemmas. Large-scale agribusinesses appear to be the only farms that can afford to sell livestock and produce at prices low enough to attract the necessary world market. However, there is the danger that, in order to do this, they may spoil the countryside in the immediate future, and ruin the land in the long term. Intensive methods that damage the ecology are often the result of the search for profit, and the insistence of paymasters that farmers grow genetically modified crops and use hormones and unnatural feeds before the possible consequences of these are fully known. Furthermore, agribusinesses need fewer and fewer employees.

Both large and small farmers have been heavily subsidized by both the European Union and the government. Unfortunately neither Conservative nor Labour Ministers of Agriculture used the BSE crisis to promote organic farming and ecologically responsible methods through the judicious manipulation of subsidies. Sheep farmers, too, were subsidized to raise many more animals than the market would absorb. At the same time the present government imposed a whole raft of new regulations on slaughterhouses, which has meant that many local concerns have had to close, and the costs of slaughtering unwanted sheep became prohibitive.

To be fair, from 1994 successive governments promoted the Organic Farming Scheme to encourage farmers to undertake the lengthy process of converting from conventional methods. The scheme was poorly funded and, alas, too popular with farmers. This was shown in April 1999, when an estimated 30,000 hectares (74,000 acres) were eligible for the new payments on offer at that time. This meant that more than half the £8.5 million budget for the following year would go to second-year payments before any new applications could be considered. Government reaction was swift. The scheme was closed down at the beginning of August.

Helen Browning, chairwoman of the Soil Association, reacted strongly: 'This news is going to put the brakes on literally thousands of British farmers who are seriously considering converting to organic farming. By inadequately funding the scheme the government has lost a crucial opportunity to revitalize the beleaguered farming industry in this country in a sector where the potential is obvious to everyone. With 70 per cent of organic food sold in the UK currently being imported, they are passing up a massive opportunity to redirect agriculture in a way that will benefit consumers, farmers and the countryside.'

Tiny handouts, such as the £10 million announced in October 1999, are footling, given the rapidly increasing public demand for organic produce, and the numbers of farmers who are eager to convert if it is economically possible.

The Common Agricultural Policy is often blamed for some of the farmers' misfortunes and certainly increased regulation, a great deal of it in the form of Whitehall 'add ons' rather than actual Brussels directives, tends to damage small farmers and businesses even more than large ones. The EU itself tends to generosity when the Treasury and the Ministry of Agriculture, Fisheries and Food are willing to facilitate matters.

The reaction of farmers' representatives to a crisis is to call for yet more subsidy and sooner or later the tax payer gets fed up. Among the population at large farmers are often viewed with exasperation. They are perceived to have brought many of their misfortunes on their own heads. Unfair this perception may be, but it does exist, and unfortunately farmers often seem to be singularly bad at marketing themselves.

According to the NFU we are facing a farming exodus on the scale of that in France, where the number of farms has fallen from two million to 700,000 in thirty years. Britain with half the landmass currently boasts 240,000 'farm businesses', so we are to expect that only about 84,000 of them will survive the next three decades.

Ben Gill, president of the National Farmers' Union, warns that from a social point of view a farming exodus 'indirectly affects local businesses, the village shop, the garage, pub, village hall and those who go to the local church and local primary school. And the closure of the local primary school is the death knell of these local communities.' Indeed yes, but these are losses which have been accelerating through agricultural booms and depressions at least since the 1970s, and bank branches and post offices have gone with them.

There is no point in resisting all change, or deploring the truth that things can no longer be done as they were in the past. It is a British characteristic, and probably a universal human one, to look back to a mythical golden age when summers were long and the world was peaceful and prosperous. In fact, as Sir Roy Strong has put it: 'The past was no better than today, just different.' The future may or may not be better, but it too will be different.

The end of farming as we have known it is not necessarily a glum prospect, however. Ideally, rather than old farmhouses and cottages filled with teleporters and surrounded by prairies managed by agribusinesses that produce unpalatable or unwanted crops, a more diverse rural society will evolve, with smaller, preferably organic, farms and farm shops and traditional businesses supporting, and being supported by, a population that derives its livelihood from sources other than the land.

# FARMLAND

Almost everyone who moves to the country is affected by farming in one way or another. Many people may find that they have acquired a parcel of farmland along with a country property, and still others may buy fields or woods in order to protect their homes from intrusive development or protect their privacy. And, of course, there is the considerable satisfaction to be gained in giving a helping hand to a neighbour from time to time. To quote T.H. White: 'One can get a lot of pleasure out of farming, if one isn't a farmer. I am neither a farmer, nor a farm labourer, so my work on the land is a pure joy.'

Catherine Paice is a leading freelance journalist specializing in agricultural and rural affairs. Here she gives an overview of farming life today for those who may not have experienced it before, but find themselves living in an agricultural community.

# Farming for Beginners

Quiet, peaceful, plenty of fresh air – yes. But much as the emphasis is now on opening up tracts of open countryside to the public, on sharing the glories of the British landscape and heritage with visitors, and on providing a showcase that demonstrates the particular arts, crafts and skills of country people, the country is fundamentally a workplace that has to earn a living for many of the 25 per cent of the population – and growing – who live in it.

With the agricultural workforce totalling no more than 600,000, few of these country dwellers farm themselves, although many more are involved in its ancillary industries. Nevertheless, over three-quarters of the countryside is still farmed – although the number of farms is in long-term decline as holdings merge and become larger in the face of intense financial pressure.

It is now a common benchmark that you need 400 arable hectares (1,000 acres) in order to make money at farming crops. A recent report by a national firm of accountants suggested that a 300 hectare (750 acre) mixed, family farm will lose, on average, £10,000 during 1999/2000. Farms are having to get bigger to survive.

The countryside as we know it has been shaped by these farmers, and anyone who moves to the countryside will find themselves particularly welcomed if they make the effort to find out how it works and can tolerate and support sensible, responsible farming practices. Some 80 per cent of the British countryside is covered by environment designations – Environmentally Sensitive Areas (ESAs), Countryside Stewardship Schemes, Habitat Schemes, Countryside Premium Schemes, Nitrate Sensitive Areas (NSAs), Nitrate Vulnerable Zones (NVZs), Farm Woodland Premium Schemes (FWPS). Many offer payments in return for farming in ways which do not damage the natural environment, and especially for restricting the use of chemical inputs.

Roughly a third of farmland is tenanted, the remainder owner-occupied – and less than 1 per cent of farmland changes hands each year.

The golden years of agriculture were from the end of the Second World War to the mid-1970s, following Britain's entry to the then European Economic Community. Successive governments encouraged ever-increasing yields until we suddenly hit the problem of overproduction. Agricultural policy today has been shaped by a twenty-five-year U-turn to the point when financial support is finally being split away from production and directed towards protecting, improving and enhancing the 'natural' features of the countryside and supporting rural communities.

In response to Government incentives, and to the credit of those who live and work the countryside, there are more areas devoted to conserving a balanced environment, more birds, more wildlife and more trees than there have been for decades.

England is, rightly, proud of the variety of its landscape. In the South-West you will still find small farms, small fields and high hedge boundaries. Even in the highly populated south-eastern Home Counties, you will still find working farms – but their numbers are dwindling fast. The eastern counties hold the vast tracts of arable land suitable for bigger, more sophisticated machinery.

England can broadly be split into areas dominated by certain types of farming, and the choice on where to live should be influenced by the environment in which you wish to find yourself.

### ARABLE FARMING

Arable farming is concentrated down the eastern side of the country. There are still many mixed farms, however, where pasture and trees are interspersed with cereal fields. Penetrating up into Cambridgeshire and Lincolnshire, you are more likely to find yourself in open, flatter tracts of vegetable and intensive arable farming country. Some people find these counties unfettered and wildly romantic; others find them downright bleak.

Francis, Earl of Bedford, and his son William, the first duke, made the drainage of the southern fenland one of their principal tasks during the seventeenth century. Their adviser in a project that would have been colossal even with modern technology was a Dutch engineer, Vermuyden. Their success fuelled further drainage projects during the eighteenth century when the northern fenland in Lincolnshire was reclaimed to create what is now some of the best arable land in Britain.

During the eighteenth century another prominent landowner in the east of the country was Viscount Townshend of Raynham, in Norfolk ('Turnip Townshend'), whose four-course rotation introduced root crops after wheat, followed by barley which was undersown with red clover and later combined with ryegrass. Norfolk still boasts some of the biggest traditional, landed estates, many of which continue to be innovative.

Wheat and barley are the principal arable crops. Nowadays, varieties may be short and stout, or long and thin – the former have been bred to resist lodging (falling down in bad weather). It's very difficult to tell wheat and barley apart – indeed it is difficult to identify any crops – when they are emerging from the ground, but once they have got going they have clear characteristics: wheat carries 'ears' full of grain; barley is hairy.

Popular 'break crops', which introduce a change to the staple crops and provide nutrition or nitrogen for the soil, are oilseed rape with its vivid yellow flowers and pungent preharvest aroma, peas, beans and the glorious billowing lilac of linseed – sadly on its way out again following a sharp reduction in EU support.

Crops are sown in the autumn or spring. One thing you won't suffer any more is the smoke from stubble-burning at the end of harvest in August. Too many people complained that it was ruining their laundry, and it has been banned.

Spraying is carried out under strict guidelines and regulations, so spray drift on windy days is far less of an irritant than it was a decade ago. Farmers spray much less, and much more efficiently, partly for environmental and partly for cost-cutting reasons.

If you decide to live in an arable area, be prepared to experience huge activity at harvest time – your lane may be blocked several times a day by combine harvesters as big as, and usually costing more than, a cottage or by grain carts hauled by huge tractors. If you are near farm buildings you may be subjected to the twenty-four-hour drone of a grain dryer. Take heart: the harvest lasts for only a few weeks of the year.

## LIVESTOCK FARMING

Heavier rainfall in the west of Britain encourages good grass, so livestock and dairy farming dominate in that part of the country. Commercial dairy breeds are mainly black-and-white – Friesian and Holstein – while favoured beef cattle are usually red, cream, roan, brown or black. Charolais (dark reddish brown), Limousin (cream), Hereford (brown and white) and Aberdeen Angus (almost black) are common beef breeds, although more traditional British breeds like the Devon (stocky and ruby-red) are popular in the West Country, and others are making a come-back.

On higher land and mountains, sheep and cattle breeding are likely to be the main enterprises, with stock crossed with lowland breeds and finished (fattened) lower down. Many hill and upland areas are designated Less Favoured Areas in recognition of the constraints put on farming by harsh natural conditions and the danger of depopulation.

Cattle thrive on grass-based diets, supplemented by cereals, kale and concentrates in the winter when they are often housed and stall-fed, or fed in yards. Calving is generally in spring or autumn – if you hear bellowing from cows at these times it is often because their calves have been removed for weaning.

Sheep, like suckler cows (reared for breeding), mix well with an arable enterprise and also survive and thrive at higher altitudes. There are hundreds of breeds and crosses, many with a local flavour and tradition. Wool is an unprofitable commodity nowadays, so farmers concentrate on breeding flocks for lamb meat.

There are certain areas of specialist interest like the concentration of pig breeders in, for example, north-east and eastern England. Outdoor pig breeding has gained enormously in popularity here where soils are drier, sandier and free-draining, and tends to create a less pervasive odour than the wafts that escape from an indoor unit. Most potent of all can be the aroma from an indoor chicken unit – check out your neighbours before you buy a property.

Smells are also pervasive when slurry is spread on mixed or live-stock farms principally in the winter, but, like all potentially offensive farming practices – which are carried out because they are good for the soil – in general they are efficiently and swiftly carried out, and the smell fades quite quickly.

Silage is now as important as hay for livestock. It is made two or three times a year, beginning in May/June and ending in September/October, and the process takes a few weeks depending on the weather and the extent of the farm's grass or maize acreage.

When you have spent some time in the countryside, you may find yourself joining the ranks of those who claim that food is too cheap – because you will have discovered why cheap food is synonymous with intensive, low-employment 'factory' farming practices. And you may realize the value of small-farming neighbours who have lived in the area for generations, and who are always there – day and night. Many incomers who do not isolate themselves, but equally do not interfere, have found that their best neighbours are considerate farming families who will not intrude, yet know everyone and their comings and goings – who should be there, and who might pose a threat to security.

## OPTIONS AND REGULATIONS

If you are not sure what you want to do with your land, talk to your neighbours and the nearest recommended firm of rural chartered surveyors or farm consultants. It may also be worth joining NFU Countryside – for members with 'small' acreages – or the Country Landowners' Association (see Directory, page 245). Both offer a wealth of information and advice.

Whether you decide to farm intensively or in a small way, or anywhere in between, remember that farming is increasingly strictly regulated. No one can dictate what you should farm, or even how you do it, but there are strict health and safety monitoring and control procedures. Organic farming is gaining ground fast – areas under conversion have tripled in 1998 and 1999 – and the government is putting more money into supporting it. It is more labour intensive than mechanized farming and requires a different approach – people who have never farmed before can be among the best organic farmers.

If you have less than a few hundred or, preferably thousand, acres it won't be worth taking on a farm manager. If you don't want to deal with the land yourself, there are a number of options. Farm business tenancy (FBT) legislation introduced in 1995 (the Agricultural Tenancies Act) allows you to let land to local farmers or growers for an agreed period – as short or long as you like – under agreed conditions. You are likely to find a good market, even for as little as 20 acres (8 hectares). Farmers are increasingly on the lookout for more land over which to spread their costs, and arable land with a capital value of £2,200 to £2,800 an acre (.4 hectares) is commonly being let for £100 per acre per annum upwards. Potato-growing land attracts a huge premium. Otherwise, local farmers or a farming company may be interested in farming the land on contract. There is a wide variety of arrangements under which this can be achieved; take time to find one which suits you.

Devolution in Scotland and Wales is likely to lead to those countries creating their own rules and regulations governing land ownership and occupation as well as farming. The Welsh Assembly, for example, has the right to change statutory law, which governs many agricultural regulations.

Whatever you decide to do, you are strongly recommended to take advice at every stage of buying, taking on, or making changes to, rural land and property. Take heart, though – we are not yet at the stage reached by some estates close to cities in northern Europe where designations have been imposed whereby the owner cannot walk his own dogs across his own land!

The following provides a brief glimpse into an immensely complicated arena.

**BIOMASS:** The Department of Trade and Industry is encouraging farmers and landowners to grow short rotation coppices (SRC), of which poplar is the most popular, as alternative energy crops. England's first power station fuelled by SRC, at Eggborough in Yorkshire, is up and running.

**BOUNDARIES:** The cause of the most common legal disputes in rural areas. If you buy into the countryside, try and make sure you are not inheriting a boundary dispute or likely to fall prey to one.

**BUILDINGS:** You may find income-earning potential in redundant farm buildings. Planning guidance is in favour of conversion to alternative business use ranging from offices to storage. Getting planning permission is not normally simple or straightforward. Plan ahead. You generally need permission to put up new farm buildings or demolish old ones.

**BUREAUCRACY:** Unavoidable, and increasing in the wake of BSE and food scares. Every farm has a holding number. Every move in the food chain is monitored. Those with arable land are required to fill in IACS (Integrated Administrative and Control System) forms annually in order to register for farm subsidies and payments. Every cow and calf has to be numbered and registered, and hold a passport if it is to be moved off the farm. And so it goes on.

**CAP:** The EU's Common Agricultural Policy dictates the structure of, and financial support for, agriculture in all member states. The EU annually spawns reams of directives and laws governing agricultural policy, health, safety and animal welfare – most of which have to be incorporated into UK law or regulations.

**DIVERSIFICATION:** You name it, you can do it – and most farmers are trying to. Buffalo (top London restaurants are buying mozzarella from British buffalo farms), deer, holiday lets, bed and breakfast. Most have their own associations.

135

**EMPLOYMENT**: Under new regulations, employees of a farm or estate which is transferring to new ownership have to be taken on by the new owner or be made redundant. Seek legal advice.

**HEALTH AND SAFETY**: Strict legislation covers health and safety in the rural workplace, at every point of the food chain and in waste disposal. There are a growing number (too many, some say) of food assurance schemes which monitor the process of food production on the farm and provide an accreditation label for the end product (see also Bureaucracy, previous page). This is a clear future path for the farming industry.

**HEDGEROWS**: Now strictly protected. You need planning permission to take out a hedgerow and will be in trouble if you do so without obtaining it.

**MAFF**: If you plan to be involved in farming to any extent you will have to make yourself known at, and get to know, your local Ministry of Agriculture, Fisheries and Food office (see Directory, page 245). You will have to tell the office what you are up to. You have to do this and will only be able to do what you want to do with its knowledge and consent.

**MILK QUOTAS**: Every producer is allocated a quota. Quotas are tradeable, through sale or leasing. If the national quota is exceeded in any given year, every dairy farmer is fined.

**SET-ASIDE**: Under EU regulations, 10 per cent of arable land must be left fallow. It cannot be grazed, but can be used for certain purposes such as growing fodder crops for livestock.

**SHEEP OR SUCKLER COW QUOTAS**: Required by every farmer who wishes to claim EU payments for financial support of livestock production.

**TAX**: There are strong tax incentives to buying, owning and passing on farmland. Check with your accountant.

**TREES**: One of the best options for small, as well as large, acreages. Only 10 per cent of Britain is afforested. Government is strongly in favour of new planting and advice and grants are available, mainly from the Forestry Authority (talk to local offices) and local authorities.

# CHAPTER EIGHT

# COUNTRY TRANSPORT

According to David Nicholson-Lord, writing in *A Vision of the Country AD 2097*: 'The fate of what we now call the countryside will depend on two crucial factors: leisure and transport. There is little doubt that on present trends, accessible countryside, which in Britain currently means the bulk of the landmass, will grow ever more raucous, cluttered and congested.' This is gloomy indeed, but one must ask, need it be so? The subject of country transport has been largely ignored for a couple of decades, but now, even if official thinking is still muddled, there is a realization that it must be addressed seriously.

In fact, the inadequacies of rural public transport have made it one of the hottest topics of political debate but, as so often in political debates, generalizations are thrown about as if they applied everywhere and to everyone. The problems of metropolitan Islington are not the same as those of urban Batheaston or Middlesborough, and the solutions to the difficulties experienced by those very different towns have no great relevance to the various needs of the inhabitants of rural Islington, Baston or Middlesmoor.

Furthermore, the interests of the inhabitants of market towns are not different just from those of city dwellers, but often also from the interests of people who live in the surrounding country-side. Many of the latter thoroughly approve of out-of-town supermarkets and shopping centres, while the former see them as sucking the life from traditional high streets and small businesses. Shopkeepers and businesses in town centres can hit back at their competitors by ensuring that adequate, reasonably priced, central parking facilities are maintained, especially close to areas that have been pedestrianized. And some town traders have suggested the taxing of parking spaces at out-of-town superstores – a development that is unlikely to win the approval of many shoppers from the countryside.

It is an inescapable fact that, now and for the foreseeable future, country people need cars more than most people who live in towns; and it is as sad a truth that many people who move to the country not only need to use their cars more, but also have to acquire more cars. Obviously this does not necessarily apply to country towns that are well provided with rail and bus services but, equally obviously, it does apply to most villages.

Not only will more members of a family want their own cars, but nannies and au pairs need transport and the possibility of a social life – or you are unlikely to get them and certainly won't keep them. Local cleaners also sometimes need lifts. Should you find yourself furnishing from country sales and antique shops (see Chapter Nine) a car will be essential.

Furthermore, the Rural Services Survey, undertaken by the now defunct Rural Development Commission in 1997, found that 43 per cent of parishes did not have a post office; 42 per cent no permanent shop; 83 per cent no permanent general practitioner; and that 91 per cent had no bank, building society or dentist. A noble effort to reverse this is currently being spearheaded by ViRSA (see Directory, page 249). Provision of childcare and similar personal services was markedly lower than in urban areas.

For all these reasons, although it goes against the ecological grain, a second vehicle may be therefore the only practical answer. Thus extra petrol, insurance and running expenses may have to be included in the long-term costs of your decision to move. In addition, as part of the process of moving, it may be sensible to consider whether you will need to change your town car for a more practical model. While most people do not actually need a four-wheel drive, a comparatively large vehicle may be advisable for bulk shopping, school runs and the general ferrying of children and dogs.

A particularly unfortunate consequence of this reliance on the car is that almost eight times as many people die in accidents on country roads and lanes as are killed on motorways. A contributory factor, of course, is the natural tendency of people who know a road well to drive fast without allowing for others who are unacquainted with local characteristics. Allowances must be made for riders, cyclists and pedestrians, and speed limits for some lanes, together with variable limits for villages, have been given serious consideration. The Council for the Preservation of Rural England (see Directory, page 248) and other associations have argued for a 20 mph limit for village traffic and the creation of 15 mph 'quiet lanes', together with 40 mph limits on designated rural roads.

One solution, which may be less utopian than it might seem, has been called 'the resocializing of the car'. In many areas there are well-established volunteer networks of car owners prepared to ferry isolated old people to local towns and shops, and further shared use, or even shared ownership, of vehicles should obviously be encouraged. These are both measures that could be formally recognized by the tax authorities, and promoted by insurers and manufacturers.

Similarly, as the Countryside Alliance argues and common sense dictates, there should be tax rebates on diesel for local taxi services. If the fiscal authorities could be persuaded to abandon their traditional suspicion of the self-employed and do away with the over-regulation of small businesses, many under- or unemployed people might be tempted to set up in business running either full- or part-time taxi services. This should keep prices within reasonable limits and be widely beneficial.

At the moment there are far too few operators – in 1999, a Women's Institute's survey of village life reported that only 38.3 per cent of respondents had a convenient local taxi service. And many of those respondents will also have less than generous bus services. As a lifelong Wiltshire villager put it: 'In the old days there were buses every hour and a half. Today there are four a week, and anyone wanting to shop in Corsham on market day has just enough time to buy a loaf before jumping back on board if they want to get home that day.'

The axing of bus services for villages and the awkward timetables of many of those that have survived have been constant subjects of complaint for years and, since privatization, the difficulties have increased for people who live near the boundaries between the territories of the various companies.

## COMMUTING

The most important factor to consider when you are looking for a property in the country is whether one or more of you will be travelling to and from work on a daily or weekly basis. I have always hated the idea of commuting, whether daily by packed rush-hour trains in the southern counties or, at the other extreme, the three- or four-day regime of a friend who divides his life between Aberdeenshire and London. He is lucky in that he can both work and think profitably when travelling. However, for many people commuting is a compromise well worth making, in order to enjoy at least something of country life, and rail, road and perhaps even air times to the city of their labours are the most important factors in deciding where they can live.

Regular rail commuters generally use car minutes to express the time it takes them to drive to the station – which should itself be no more than about an hour from their work. The consensus is that ten to fifteen car minutes is best. Inevitably, such a constraint may mean you have to forego the utopian property of your dreams. Prices also naturally go up within the magic fifteen-car-minute radius.

It is vital to understand the costs that are likely to be involved, particularly if you will be commuting by rail. As a London couple who were defeated by a move to Sussex put it: 'Our excited back-of-an-envelope calculations had not included train fares. It is one thing to give up a flat at £650 a month in Fulham for a house at £750 near Brighton – but £400 in train fares needed to be added to the rent.' In 1998 an annual season ticket cost £2,400 from Ashford in Kent, where car parking at the station added a further £265 per annum; and £1,748 from Sevenoaks, where the shorter railway journey (only thirty-five minutes) was reflected in higher property prices.

In one important respect buses, or rather coaches, are a great deal better than trains. In some areas regular commuters find that it is considerably cheaper to band together to charter a coach up to town rather than continuing to use rail services. An acquaintance who travels between the north Kent coast and London each day rebelled when the price of his rail season ticket rose to £2,200. His travelling companions agreed with him and now his share of a reliable coach, which drops him conveniently close to his office and is waiting for him in the evening, costs him £900 a year. He is guaranteed a seat; it is comfortable; and it leaves, and usually arrives, on time.

He is fortunate in that he works regular hours. However, not everyone can leave their job at the same time each day. If this applies to you, remember that it is one thing to endure the crowds on the six o'clock train with the thought of dinner to sustain you, and quite another to fall on to the last train – which may be a stopper with changes – at 10.30 pm, leaving you little time to sleep before getting up again.

# THE INTERNET FOR COUNTRY TRAVELLERS

In the course of compiling this book I have acquired mountains of local bus timetables from almost all the companies (see Directory, page 245) – and come to the conclusion that it would be a brave and remarkably patient person who used them to plan any long or complicated journey. However, help is increasingly to be found on the Internet.

At present there is one web directory (see Directory, page 245), which is the key for information on public transport in the UK and covers all travel by rail, air, coach, bus, ferry, metro and tram, including the links with Ireland. It is the definitive index to timetables, fares, ticket types, passenger facilities and much more and is linked to many other relevant web sites. A word of warning: if you go straight to some of the telephone numbers you will be charged at premium rates.

The web directory opens with a number of options, including a search facility and area maps within which any form of transport can be investigated. Otherwise you can go directly to express coach travel; rail travel; air travel; ferry travel; national phone hotline; leisure trips by public transport; and major transport groups.

This web site is bound to be joined by others within a short time, and it will become easier not only to plan journeys, but also to reserve and pay for seats online rather than by telephone or in person.

# SHANKS'S AND OTHER PONIES

There are no easy solutions to transport problems in rural areas. Certainly, it is no answer to build more roads, and as futile to try to cut the numbers of cars by high taxes. It is essential that matters are not allowed to drift for much longer but, until a strategy that is both wide-ranging and sensitive to the needs of small communities and individuals is produced, there is little helpful advice that can be offered.

However, there are many people living in the countryside who escape the frustrations of travelling by public transport, and whose lives are, for this reason, utterly enviable. They are the lucky souls whose workplaces are close enough to their homes for them to be able to use more old-fashioned forms of locomotion. Walkers and cyclists are also common enough in towns, but I have known country people who ride to work as a matter of course, others who walk through fields and one who, until recently, travelled by pony and trap on busy roads in Hertfordshire. Perhaps the most enviable lot of all is that of an architect acquaintance who is able to commute between his home on the River Dart and his office in Totnes aboard his sturdy fishing boat. It would be paradise indeed were he able to catch the supper on the way home.

# CHAPTER NINE

# SOCIAL LIFE, EDUCATION AND COUNTRY CONCERNS

A most important piece of advice for anyone settling into a new country home is: work at your social life, but don't rush things. Many people find it quite usual to make instant best friends in the course of urban life. A chance meeting at a city party, or when walking the dog or airing children in the park, can lead rapidly to warm neighbourliness and genuine friendship. If relations do not flourish it is comparatively easy to let them wither. In the country getting to know people usually takes longer, if only because it is less simple to drop an acquaintanceship.

A French friend, who was brought up in a village in the Vendée, says the best advice he ever had came from his father as he was leaving to work for a year in the Suffolk town of Lavenham: 'Don't say anything'. By this, his father meant that he should be friendly but reserved up to a point, and unpushing. This could be amplified as: 'Remember that a village or small town has its gossips'.

In most places the pub, if there still is one, along with the church, provides a useful place to introduce yourself to the neighbourhood. Happily, almost everywhere the pub has lost its reputation as a bastion of silent and unwelcoming villagers. Society has become more fluid over the years, football provides a common subject of conversation for many and newcomers are not as rare as they once were. To illustrate the point, I remember that when my father and I went into a pub in Suffolk, many years ago, the place fell silent until we left. We were made very welcome a day or two later when we were taken in by a friend who was well known in the county – and one of the last speakers of Suffolk dialect. However, our friend warned us that should we go back unaccompanied, the same people would freeze us out once more. The pub is still there, and now has a friendly welcome for all – visitors and locals alike.

## CONTACTS AND CONNECTIONS

Inevitably any contacts you already have in a neighbourhood will affect the way you are received, either for good or ill. A couple who rented a country house told me: 'We were lucky in that our landlord is very popular, and this rubs off in the way we have been welcomed.' On the other hand, I recall three family holidays in an East Anglian village. During the first two summers we were in a large thatched cottage owned by an antique dealer, but people hardly nodded and we got to know virtually no one. The third visit was to a cottage with a sociable and well-liked owner, and on the first morning we had three callers asking us to drinks or offering the use of a tennis court. I sometimes wonder what the dealer had done to offend her neighbours.

The best piece of advice offered by an observer of social movements in Devon, which actually applies to many other parts of the country and indeed chimes with that given to my French friend, is twofold:

1   Don't try to import a purely London lifestyle with no conces-
    sions to locality – fashionably metropolitan sponged walls
    don't much suit traditional farmhouses. Whether true or *ben
    trovato*, poor Peter Mandelson will never escape the story of
    how he mistook mushy peas for avocado dip in a Northern
    working men's club.

2   Contrariwise, be yourself wherever you settle. Trying too
    hard to be local merely irritates. In Devon not long ago, a
    smooth young political operator won few friends by standing
    for the district council within six months of his arrival. His
    new neighbours quite understandably suspected that they
    were being used as stepping stones to a House of Commons
    seat. His Devon longhouse walls were sponged.

Of course, the right sort of pushiness can do the trick, but not
everyone can hope to get it right. Some acquaintances made the
move across the Welsh border from Hereford to Powys – a much
greater distance than the map suggests. The parish and town councils were keen to sell an historic treasure from the fine local church
in order to install lavatories inside it, but the incomers forcefully
joined their voices to the opposition. The matter generated a great
deal of heat, and their 'foreign' status was pointedly alluded to.

Shortly afterwards a workman armed with a chainsaw was
discovered about to cut down a fine and healthy magnolia in
front of their house. He had been ordered to do this, he said, by
the town council, because the tree was dangerous. He was
persuaded to go away while enquiries were made, but the council
was gleefully adamant that the tree must be felled. However, the
tables were turned by a successful application to the council's
own planning department for a tree preservation order. This exercise in barrack-room legalism caused much amusement and has
ensured that the incomers are now thoroughly welcome.
Furthermore, the church was dissuaded from parting with its
treasure, which is now proudly and properly displayed for the
enjoyment – and financial benefit – of the community.

It is sad that the practice of 'calling' and leaving cards has long died out. It was a form of measured welcome that indicated that neighbours were there and prepared to help and be friendly, but did not commit anyone to premature intimacy. In Languedoc, and for all I know elsewhere in rural France, a newcomer is expected to take the initiative and ask the neighbours in for a drink. People who are unaware of this custom think the natives are being stand-offish, while the natives consider them unmannerly. In England it is more common for an incomer to wait to be invited by the neighbours; to issue the first invitation might be construed as being pushy.

Of course, pushiness works in both directions. A fellow property journalist complicated her life considerably a year or two ago. Her career was entirely London-based and she was by way of being an atheist. Not only did she engage herself to a country vicar, but – reader, she married him!

Since this was a distinctly modern marriage she was the one who made the weekly commute and spent the weekends at his place of work. As it happened, she had a friend who had also become a vicar's wife who, when the news of the engagement broke, rang with a cryptic, but invaluable, piece of advice: 'Beware the bringers of strawberries.'

The truth and value of this became apparent as early as the first affianced weekend. There were regular knocks on the back and front doors as a stream of parishioners arrived to welcome and assess the new unstipended help. All brought a little something, here a cake, there a pot of chutney – it happened not to be the strawberry season. As her friend had implied, and as my journalist friend's future husband was sadly able to confirm, most had campaigns to wage and were eager to enlist her support.

# CHILDREN AND SCHOOLS

Together with enhancing the quality of life, the determination to obtain the best education for their children is one of the main reasons why many people move out of town. It is easy enough nowadays to get information on the rankings and performance of schools around the country, and the various league tables are extensively published in the press. What may be a little more difficult, is getting the local word on which primary schools are particularly well regarded in their areas. These are not always the ones at the top of official lists. For this reason the educational information in the county profiles in Chapter 10 has been largely restricted to noting the outstanding state primary schools.

State, private or a mixture, boarding, weekly boarding or day, these are entirely matters for individual choice. The educational needs of the children must be paramount, and decisions about them are private and personal matters. Upon your choice, however, may depend not only the location of your home but perhaps also the course of your social life.

It must be said that 'empty nesters' are at a disadvantage when it comes to making friends, since babies or small children perform a useful social function in allowing perfect strangers to stop and make conversation with their parents. Similarly, incomers who come provided with school-age children have a key to social life that is not available to others. The selection of a primary school is more than just an educational choice. A decision in favour of a village primary will gain you local acceptance more quickly, but a day or boarding prep school will attract people from a wider area, and expand your choice of potential friends among other parents. Local schools may be excellent for you and your children's needs at present – even though they are not always that local as many have amalgamated with schools in neighbouring villages – but present convenience must not blind you to longer term considerations, social as well as educational.

Children tend to grow up and, as they do, their social lives will require yet more driving time from you if they are not to be terminally bored. Your home may be perfect for a primary or prep school, but how well placed will it be when the move on to secondary education has to be faced? At that point, or rather before, you must discover whether you – and your child – are prepared to consider boarding. Even if you would rather not send your child to boarding school you may find that you just do not have time to be a full-time chauffeur. It is a question of what best suits the character of the individual child – and what you are able to cope with, mentally and financially. All these are matters which it is important to check out and consider carefully before you move to the country. The alternative to boarding could be another move, just when you have put down your fresh roots.

Whether you decide for state or public education, the hierarchies of the school may very well influence your relationships with other parents: just as children mainly make friends with pupils in their own year, so their parents tend to socialize with the parents of these friends. People who have already established themselves don't always remember that newer newcomers may need a helping hand. A cautionary tale is of a newly arrived mother who asked a longer established school parent to supper: 'No thank you,' was the practical but ungracious and hubristic reply. 'I've got enough friends already.'

I am told that a similar unwritten law governs that still earlier source of young parental social life: the Natural Childbirth Trust class. Bonding tends to be between first-timers, and friendships are seldom established between them and women who have already had children.

As long as you have the transport and the stamina there is usually a great deal of choice for out-of-school activities. Pony clubs (see opposite and Directory, page 250), Scout and Guide groups and all sorts of sporting clubs are an excellent source of enjoyment and generally widely available, and will allow you a few days' break in the school holidays.

Life in the country is not, of course, only about schools, children's activities and your own social life and there are many pleasures to be enjoyed, either alone or with other people. There are parts of the country where the traditional sport is hunting, and where it is impossible to ignore the passions that this inspires. Here, however, I concentrate on the horses, whether you hunt them or not, and on another popular country pursuit: walking.

# GOOD HORSEKEEPING

Like marriage, equine ownership is 'not by any to be enterprised, nor taken in hand, unadvisedly, lightly or wantonly... but reverently, discreetly, advisedly, soberly' and in the full understanding that it will be time consuming and very, very expensive.

At the very least you will need an acre or more of paddock for adequate grazing, constant fresh water and good shelter in summer as well as winter: horses may get sunburnt, especially around the nose, and they can suffer badly from flies and midges. When they are out, fields and stables must be mucked out.

If you think you can look after a pony or two while running a business from home, doing the school runs and shopping trips and maintaining something like sanity, think again. As a rule of thumb every horse requires at least an hour of your time every day, from the early hours of the morning (feeding it and mucking out the stables and field) through to the evening hours (washing mud off its feet, preparing feed for the morning, cleaning, clearing and checking). And all that without even riding the animal. Bits must be washed every day, and the rest of the tack at least wiped down – with a strip clean at least once a week.

Over and above hard feed, the sort of expenses and essential requirements that you must expect include shoeing (perhaps £50 per animal every five weeks), vet's bills (up to £30 per month), dentist's bills (£30 a time), hay (£2 to £5 per bale depending on the season), straw (£1 per bale) and wood shavings (£5 per bag).

And this is only the beginning: buckets, forks and feed bins will have to be replaced more frequently than you would expect and a good supply of rugs (including quilted ones for winter) will be necessary. You will also need electric fencing to prevent the animals overgorging on rich grass – and be prepared to pull out ragwort, which is poison to stock of any kind, by the roots. Should you take up hunting or competing, your expenses will increase considerably.

Just as with houses, this should prompt the question: do you actually need to buy? One option might be to share the ownership of a horse with another enthusiast. At the very least it might be sensible to hire a horse for a trial period. This should at least ensure that you have a quiet, reliable animal and you must insist on a formal legal contract setting out who is financially responsible for what, including insurance, medical bills and the like.

Similarly, if you do decide to buy, do be careful. In horse-coping all is fair, and someone who stitches you up is only to be congratulated. A phrase to beware in advertisements is 'well-hunted'. This should mean well mannered and experienced, but check with your local hunt and the Pony Club (see Directory, page 250) for independent eyewitnesses to its behaviour. And remember that a reputable seller – caveat emptor – should give you a one- or two-week trial period with the animal against a deposit.

The Pony Club, which has 364 branches in the United Kingdom, is a practical entrée to local social life for parents as well as their children. There are also numerous associated activities which require voluntary helpers.

# WALKING

One of the pleasures of being in the country is the possibility of walks, brisk or otherwise – and another is saying no to one on a cold, grey afternoon after a good lunch when it is beginning to drizzle and there is an inviting fire to snooze by.

However, even on a drab winter afternoon there is much to notice during a walk through fields and woods and as the natural and farming years unfold there is more and more to enjoy. Some people become naturalists almost without intending to, and are soon able to recognize not only crops and trees, but the calls of birds and tracks of animals; others become archaeologists, able to read a landscape and its history. Yet others seek more immediate gratification, picking blackberries and sloes or – after buying a reliable guide and taking local advice – edible fungi.

A practical study for new country people is meteorology. As T.H.White wrote in *England Have My Bones*: 'Clouds are an interesting hobby for anybody who lives in the country, because they have a direct bearing on the weather, like the wind.' Of the four main kinds: the wispy, high-flying cirrus means dry weather; the heaped soap suds of cumulus also means fair weather; misty, horizontal stratus is related to fog; and grey, horizontal, jagged, formless, mobile nimbus betokens rain or snow.

As you get to know your part of the country you will soon learn where neighbouring landowners are happy for you to walk and pick, and where it is tactful not to venture. Obviously you must not harm crops or worry livestock, and gates must be closed. It also makes sense to teach yourself to recognize which cattle are safe to walk among, and which might be dangerous.

A dog or a puppy will add to your enjoyment. The latter need not be fully trained when it is too young to worry pheasants or strip bantams, but must be later if it is not to grow from a charming advantage to a drawback. If a dog turns into a sheep-worrier, for instance, a responsible animal-loving owner must ensure that it cannot get out as there is the risk that it may be shot.

Treasure-seeking, although not perhaps a major concern for many people, is a potential source of friction: over the years amateur archaeologists, especially those armed with metal detectors, have destroyed crops, and damaged walls, hedges or fences and there have been acrimonious disputes about the ownership of finds. Until recently a landowner might have a claim to anything found on his land and it was sometimes worth a finder's while to sell treasure – essentially, gold and silver objects and coins over 300 years old that had been buried with the intention of recovery, whose owner or his heirs cannot be traced – illicitly, rather than reporting and recording what he had found. The new Treasure Act makes it more likely that a finder who has reported his find will be awarded it, while still safeguarding the rights of landowners.

## ACCESS OR TRESPASS

Given that responsible walkers will always respect the land and property of farmers and other landowners, the question remains: where exactly *should* people be allowed to walk? The campaign by the Ramblers' Association and others for 'the right to roam' has generated a great deal of heat, and resulted in an announcement that the government will introduce a general statutory right of access to open countryside. In addition to the existing 119,000 miles of public footpaths, it proposes opening up a further 7,400,000 acres of open countryside (moor, mountain, heath and common land) to the public. This barely affects lowland farming, but could be the start of something much bigger. As a country dweller, you will have a legs-on opportunity to contribute to the ongoing public access debate.

The dilemma was well expressed in a letter to the *Guardian* in June 1998: '... Suckler cows are dangerous. In this part of the Yorkshire Dales, a nearby farm has only two fields without public footpaths through them. On most weekends hundreds of walkers go through the farmyard. Somehow the farmer must protect the animals from the people – and the people from the animals. So, like all farmers, our friend keeps paying his insurance...'

It is perhaps relevant to note that the Gallup/Strutt & Parker survey of February 1999 (see Introduction) found that 63 per cent of respondents, drawn evenly from town and country, did not feel unduly restricted when walking in the countryside. This would suggest that rather than blanket legislation, problems should be addressed, as they arise, at the local level.

The report concludes that: 'The fear must be that an unqualified right of access ignores the majority's real priorities in the countryside and could create environmental "flash points" where wildlife and crops are damaged due to central legislation which cannot predict local implications. The extent of powers for Local Access Fora in safeguarding the countryside will be crucial and in the years before legislation local concerns – including Sites of Special Scientific Interest and publicising of access – must be addressed.' 'Is it Right to Roam' (see page 156) reflects the views of a keeper in County Durham and a land agent in West Sussex.

It must be emphasized that the debate is by no means a straightforward skirmish in the class war, if such a thing still exists, and that it is often not the owners of large estates who are pitted against the ramblers. Michael Wood, a solicitor who founded the Countryside Rights Association as a result of the amount of work he was doing for other people on rights of way, notes that 'a lot of small landowners are driven to despair, and they are not the land barons'.

A case which points up the problems that can be faced by people who would not consider themselves even small landowners was given a certain amount of publicity at the beginning of 1999. It concerned an Essex village quite close to Great Dunmow, where a number of paths, formerly used by mill workers, now run through private gardens with the result that many residents felt their privacy had been invaded.

Councils decide whether or not highway rights exist and if land has passed by inheritance it may well be that no searches have been undertaken for generations. It is up to an owner to prove that there is no right of way, and this can be punitively expensive in legal fees. The Ramblers' Association would like to see a compulsory question on rights of way in all property searches. Meanwhile, it has said that if an inconvenient right does

# Is it Right to Roam?

*COUNTRY LIFE*, RACHEL THOMAS, 10 JUNE 1999

'The best conservationists are keepers,' Nick Walmsley, head keeper of the Weardale estate, County Durham, asserts. 'My main aim is to preserve the land not to make money. During the season, we have only one or two days' shooting for red grouse each week and earnings from this only just cover costs.'

The worry that Mr Walmsley and other land managers have is that the government's proposed right-to-roam legislation would undermine their efforts by allowing indiscriminate access to lands that they are responsible for conserving, creating an unstoppable tide of environmental damage.

At various times of the year, Weardale is home to merlins, oyster-catchers, plovers and curlews, as well as black and red grouse, and maintaining an environment that fosters such diverse birdlife requires the efforts of three full-time keepers. The woodlands provide essential cover for deer and other participants in the complex food chain, including those less desirable predators. 'Foxes have a tough time here,' Mr Walmsley says.

What those unfamiliar with countryside management rarely understand, he believes, is that few landscapes today are the result of nature continuing unchecked. Nor are visitors always in tune with the seasonal rhythms of wildlife and their habitats. Few appreciate the impact that careless or simply naïve actions can have on the environment.

Mr Walmsley rarely warns off winter walkers who take advantage of the estate's network of footpaths, although cross-country skiers have a habit of 'accidentally' straying from the snow-hidden routeways. 'We're lucky up here that, nine-tenths of the time, the weather is dreadful, so no one comes!' he says.

But as spring advances, the barren landscape's appeal softens and Mr Walmsley faces the challenge of keeping people away from nesting hens without disturbing them himself. 'It's only in summertime that I chase people about,' he laughs. By autumn, however, the problem is not only a matter of not disturbing birds pre-shoot, but also of gun safety – added to the everyday threats of exposure, accident and the possibility of falling through the rotten boards covering one of the many shafts of former tin mines that litter the historic landscape.

The indications that leisure users will not just observe but interfere with the countryside are already plain to see, he says. The coast-to-coast mountain bike route, part of which passes through the 2,300-foot-high estate straddling County Durham, Northumberland and Cumbria has brought particular problems. 'I have never known so much litter being left,' Mr Walmsley says, pointing to the empty plastic bottles flung at the side of the road. 'It annoys me that the council doesn't clean it up.'

Education may be the answer to much of the threat to the landscape. However, this should be the job, not just of the landowners, says Captain Nigel Pease, a nearby farmer, but also of local councils and the pressure groups that fought for the right to roam. 'The Ramblers' Association must be helpful and not too radical, or there will be no cooperation,' he says. 'The government's decision to back right to roam was a marvellous vote-catcher, but the administrative detail and simply running the thing are going to be horrendous.'

Three hundred miles south, Nigel Draffan, land agent for the Goodwood Estate in West Sussex, and a member of the South Downs Conservation Board, reiterates the need to get to the nitty-gritty. 'It's time for the political dogma to end. We've got to get down to definitions – mapping, compensation and legal liabilities,' he says. Until the detail is sorted out, he argues, landowners will be watching and waiting rather than committing to further voluntary access. The longer the period of uncertainty, the more the public will lose out.

Located close to the tourist areas of Chichester and Bognor Regis and offering easily accessible vistas of rolling landscape dotted with castles of mythical beauty, the South Downs are already a magnet for lovers of the countryside. The majority of this Area of Outstanding Natural Beauty is in private hands, yet shared voluntarily with locals and visitors alike by owners willing to allow extensive and good-quality access. On the 8,000-acre Angmering Park Estate, formerly part of the Duke of Norfolk's land at Arundel in West Sussex, there are already 44 miles of footpaths, and the owners have created parking areas at the confluence of popular routes suitable for the 80,000 to 100,000 people who visit the estate annually.

Many locals derive not only pleasure but a living from the landscape whose beauty, as in Weardale, owes more to its management than may be apparent. Mr Draffan explains: 'The single issue for the Downs is to preserve their beauty. To prevent the invasion of scrub, the land has to be grazed by cattle and sheep. So it must be fenced, and therefore restricted to walkers, otherwise they will no longer find the landscape they wish to see.'

The government has suggested that areas of 'extensive grazing' may be exempted from the right to roam. But it is unclear exactly what this means, and Mr Draffan is unconvinced that walkers can distinguish between one land use and another anyway. 'To those who have no farming, botanical or scientific background, one bit of grass looks much like another,' he argues.

He also doubts the real need to extend access beyond the existing rights of way on the Downs. 'I hardly see anyone walking the footpaths midweek. At the weekend it is busier – although this is seasonal. I don't think it's a matter of there not being enough rights of way, rather that people need a better sense of where they are and where they go to.' People should also understand why rights of way first came about, he says. Originally created to offer farmworkers the shortest route from their cottages to their place of work, the paths were not intended for leisure use, nor to accommodate modern farming practices.

Disturbing the game – mostly partridges and pheasants – before a day's shoot on the Angmering Park Estate impacts not only on the wildlife and management of the bird population, but also on local employment, he points out. About thirty people may be needed to support just one shoot. Similarly, at nearby Goodwood, it is imperative that stalkers taking a shot from their high seat in the early hours do not run the risk of hitting stray walkers. 'If there is unfettered right to roam,' says Mr Draffan, 'they will not be guaranteed a safe shot, and their purpose of being there – to preserve a strong and healthy stock – will be destroyed.' Unchecked the deer population could decimate crops and new plantation of trees and leave the land unable to sustain them or other wildlife.

At present the cost of supervising existing visitors on defined areas is acceptable, Mr Draffan says. But, asked if it would ever be possible fully to monitor the activities of increased numbers exercising their right to roam, he says wryly: 'Yes, with an army of rangers at a cost of £15,000 apiece, plus a vehicle each, and housing...'

Fundamentally Mr Draffan believes the introduction of an enforced right to roam 'strikes at the core of Britons' rights to quiet enjoyment of their own property' and notes that there have been suggestions that such an infringement of historical rights should be put before the European Court of Human Rights. The irony, he says, is that landowners have always been willing to set the lead in welcoming people on to their land. 'In fifteen years here, I have hardly ever been asked by a member of the public or other organization to expand the existing rights of way networks or provide more facilities for the public. The initiative has always come from the owner or agent. It is a slow and evolving exercise.'

exist, and the owner is able to suggest a viable alternative, his proposals will be considered.

If walking is a serious matter for you, the Ramblers' Association (see Directory, page 250) has details of some 400 local rambling and hiking clubs throughout Britain.

# ANTIQUE HUNTING

Hunting out antiques and getting to know the local trade is often a sensible and pleasurable way of furnishing after a move to what may be a larger house. Thanks partly to the publicity skills of the auction houses, and partly to the enduring popularity of *The Antiques Roadshow,* antiques have become a national obsession on a par with celebrity chefs and animal hospitals. People who have always enjoyed sniffing out bargains in obscure shops and country sale rooms regret this, because there is now much more competition for an ever-decreasing stock. However, there are still occasional bargains, and the thrill of the chase is no less.

An acquaintance of mine who moved to a village near a well-known boys' public school was able to buy perfectly good furniture for spare and children's bedrooms, and other parts of the house, in the August chattels auctions at a local saleroom. At the end of each school year housemasters cleared out furniture that had been abandoned by leaving pupils or seemed otherwise past its prime. The pieces may have been distressed, but quite enough was recoverable to make it worthwhile for beady locals to note sale dates before planning their summer holiday. Similarly, military bases and other institutions with sizeable migratory populations may lead to sale-room or car boot finds. On the other hand, where large American bases survive they tend to put up prices at nearby auctions because service families seek antique souvenirs to take home.

In summer it can be worthwhile attending minor furniture and furnishing sales in London and other centres as at least some of the traders who regularly make the prices take a break then.

Contents sales in farmhouses and other country properties are also good hunting grounds, although they tend to be well publicized nowadays. Prices at major country house sales organized by the London auction houses tend to run riot and these are not occasions for bargain hunters, although they are great fun.

The (only just) subliminal message of television programmes like *The Antiques Roadshow*, with their repeated 'and at auction it might make...', obscures the role of the dealers who make up the bulk of the business. The best are more knowledgeable than many auctioneers – naturally, since they are putting their own money where their mouths are. As a result, if you are selling rather than buying, a good dealer may well pay you over the putative auction price.

The codes of practice promulgated by the major national, regional and specialist trade associations now have real teeth, and the tyro should feel much more comfortable doing business with a member of the British Antique Dealers' Association, LAPADA, the Society of London Art Dealers, the Cotswold Antique Dealers' Association and their fellows, than when chancing his arm at an auction.

During booms in the market, dealers' prices are often lower than those trumpeted at auction – they need liquidity if they are to acquire fresh stock, and are not going to up the price on long-held items after every auction of something similar (unlike stocks and shares, no two antiques or works of art are exactly the same). Equally, when the market is depressed they still need cash and are likely to be open to offers.

# GOING TO THE SHOW

Throughout summer large and small shows are held up and down the country, from prestigious events at county showgrounds to local affairs with beer tents and terrier races, and open days at agricultural colleges. Grandest of all is the annual Game Fair.

There is an immense amount to entertain even the unagricultural and unsporty. It is also no bad thing to learn more about the activities and industries that surround you in your new home. These occasions also provide excellent opportunities for meeting people and making contacts with useful trades and businesses. There may also be stands run by local and national societies that cover all sorts of activities and interests that you might wish to take up. If possible it is a good idea to go to your first few shows with a longer established friend who will be able to make the introductions. And, as ever, a well-trained dog is a good adjunct that will help to break the ice when you meet strangers.

The membership fee for the Countryside Alliance (see Directory, page 249) is worth it for its *Members' Handbook & Trade Directory* alone. It contains an unrivalled range of expertise and specialities from horse walkers to furniture makers and jewellers, and many of the trade members exhibit at county and local shows.

Local bonfire night fireworks displays, harvest festivals, carol services, music and literary festivals, flower shows, charity events and so on should also be approached with enthusiasm, even if you would not previously have considered them your sort of thing. You may very possibly discover that they are great fun. The only drawback might be that, having shown your eagerness to join in, you could find yourself pressed to serve on committees and organize many more things than you bargained for.

# CHAPTER TEN

# COUNTY SURVEY: MYTHS AND REALITIES

Thank heavens, people are different, and places are as varied as people. This may be obvious, but failure to consider these differences is often the principal cause of an unsatisfactory move – a point that I have made before in the course of this book, but one which is important enough to bear reiterating. It would be eccentric to settle in, say Bembridge or Seaview on the Isle of Wight if you have no interest in sailing, or in a village near Newbury if racehorses and their bloodlines hold no appeal. Not just neighbouring counties, but areas within counties, can differ greatly as much from the social point of view as topographically. A place may very well show different aspects at different times of year – a Cornish Christmas, for example, would not prepare you for the roads in summer – and the attitude of its inhabitants towards incomers may only become apparent after you have settled there.

It is easy to make too much of the time it takes for newcomers to be accepted by country people. Even traditionally suspicious areas are much more open nowadays, when people travel widely,

163

and it is rare to find anybody who has spent all their life in the same place. Acceptance may not be immediate, however, and you may never be accepted as fully as if you had been born and bred in the area: a scion of one of the most ancient of Cumberland's old families is said to have encountered a faint reserve when he retired full of honours to his ancestral village, because of the unfortunate fact that he had actually been born in London.

Understanding what motivates other people may take time, but from the outset it is as well to be honest about oneself. The choice of living in a village or in an isolated country property could be vital to happiness. Also, can you take a daily or weekly commute, and can the rest of the family take what may be a lonely existence?

This survey is intended to indicate some of the less tangible divisions that are part of the character of an area, but which may not be obvious at first to an incomer. Sometimes they are based on physical features of the landscape, and sometimes by man-made barriers such as canals, railways and motorways. Sometimes they may go back to ancient tribal, feudal or county boundaries that have lingered in the communal subconscious, and sometimes to modern factors such as the limits of bus company franchises.

I am not certain of the origin of the instinctive separateness of a group of neighbouring villages along the Cotswold escarpment near Broadway. It may just be the division, commented on by a number of writers, between the people of the Gloucestershire hills and the inhabitants of the valleys. The villages of Buckland and Laverton, which nestle in combes above the A46, are nowadays linked in a joint parish with communities a mile or two below, on the other side of the road, but I am told that there is hardly any social intercourse across the divide, and that there never has been. It would be unfortunate to choose one of these villages so as to be near friends who live beyond the A46. There is a modern division up the escarpment in the other direction: the railway station at Moreton-in-Marsh is only about ten miles from Broadway, but a bus runs between the two towns only twice a week because of a franchise boundary. Thus Broadway tends to look to Cheltenham, and Moreton to Oxford.

Although the following profiles of counties and areas are based on a formula – which includes, where relevant, schools from the top 500 state primaries – there are differences of emphasis and tone, just as there are within the areas. In the text I have occasionally referred to the traditional counties rather than the newly-defined unitary authorities as for practical and psychological reasons they are still important, and often more familiar. In addition, the maps illustrating this section are to give a general guide to the county boundaries rather than to illustrate in detail every town or village given. They also illustrate the most up-to-date definitions of unitary authorities and counties (as given at the time of publication).

Some places I know well through personal experience, with others I am less well acquainted, and in all cases I have pestered friends and informants for knowledge, views and observations. Naturally they have not all responded in identical ways. By no means everyone will agree with my, or their, opinions, but such things must be subjective to a certain extent. Some sources are openly acknowledged in the text, others may be grateful for a figleaf of anonymity.

The prejudices and caricatures that introduce the profiles are my own doing. Many of them are the grossest libels, but their purpose – other than giving me some fun – is to encourage settlers to consider people as well as places. It is up to you whether you agree or violently disagree. Many a myth has some basis in truth after all, and not all 'known facts' are as true as they should be; as that wise poet Richard Le Gallienne sadly wrote: 'For all is not Bass that is bottled, And all is not pork that is pie.'

# THE SOUTH-WEST

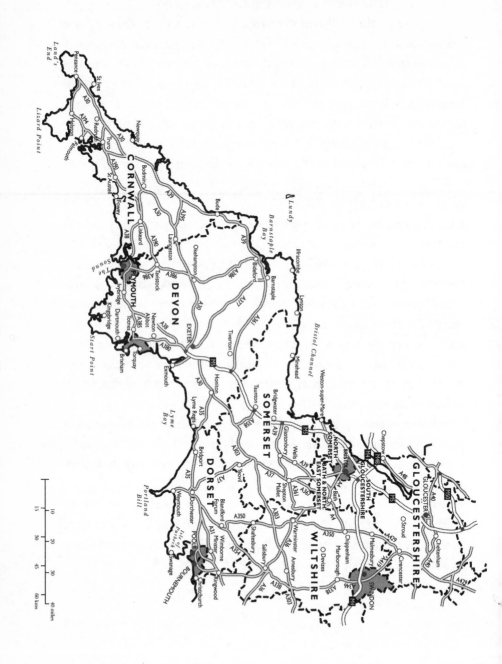

# CORNWALL

*'A very odd place, and not only because for the Cornish even Devonians are suspiciously foreign. The north Cornish coast is hearty with surfers; the south haunted by colonies of painters and, no doubt, wreckers. In between is a sleepy land with a dead language and zombies clambering out of long-disused tin mines. The living are mostly retired, gorging on disappointing pasties and rich cream. When awake the natives are prone to riotous furry dances. The place is either full of tourists or empty.'*

The north and south coasts of Cornwall, the Betjeman and du Maurier coasts, have very different characters. The softer south has sunlit bays and estuaries, the north rugged cliffs and sandy beaches; taken as a whole the coastline is one of the most varied and beautiful in Europe. Truro, with a population of under 20,000, is the smallest city in England and the second smallest in the United Kingdom. Bath-like in architecture, it is 'becoming quite cosmopolitan, with a pleasant combination of multinational and local shops', according to Jonathan Haward of Country Homesearch International, which is based there. Inland are Wadebridge and Bodmin, where there are 'discreetly wealthy indigenous communities'. There are many fine restaurants in the duchy, and much more than pasties is on offer.

Summer and winter are very different: in summer you may meet very few Cornish people other than those directly engaged in the tourist industry, while in winter they may seem to be talking among themselves as they enjoy the relief of having their place to themselves. However, it is a relaxed society, and it is easy to vegetate.

Helicopters flying in and out of RAF Culdrose may obtrude. On peak holiday weekends there is considerable traffic congestion, and there can be road noise near major routes. Wet summer weekends are the worst of all.

The granite and the slatey, metallic-looking rock of the far south-west are intractable materials, so building stones are often used in rough condition. An attempt to find a more easily worked material resulted in the masdic block – a sort of breeze block made from powdered clay and slag – used around Mousehole early in the twentieth century. Unfortunately it does not keep out salt sea winds. Other cottages are built of cob with rendered and painted walls. There are areas of thatch. Housing in the old tin-mining areas such as Camborne and Redruth ranges from terraced cottages to detached stone-built houses, reflecting the hierarchy of the eighteenth- and nineteenth-century tin industry. Grand houses are comparatively rare, but there are some sizeable rectories. In the 1960s there were serious outbreaks of bland bungalow building, but planning controls have been effective in preventing more of them.

# DEVON

*'Devonians subsist on cream teas and scrumpy – except in Plymouth where gin is swilled. Dartmoor is alive with escaping prisoners and slavering hounds, while Totnes and Dartington are magnets for ageing hippies and crafty folk. Drake is never forgotten.'*

East of the M5, the area around Honiton looks as much to Dorset and Somerset as to the rest of Devon and has a high proportion of retired people. The great brown stretch of Dartmoor, all 365 square miles (945 square kilometres) of it, is a world away from the South Hams and steeply wooded estuaries on the one side, and the central plain running north-east from Exeter on the other. Much of Dartmoor north of the Postbridge road is closed because of army firing ranges. The north coast with its cliffs is markedly different from the south, and Exmoor – the home of Tarka the otter as well as the hound of the Baskervilles – is another world of its own

It is possible to enjoy nights without a background noise of traffic or aircraft, and in most places the stars are gloriously visible. However, two beaches on the north coast and four on the south failed to reach the 1999 European Union minimum standard of purity. The north is distinctly wetter, but Devon is a county of microclimates, especially where rainfall is concerned. One place may have 37 inches (94 centimetres) per year, another five miles (8 kilometres) away suffers glumly under 75 inches (190 centimetres). Ask the locals.

Architecture, building materials and types of house vary from thatched Devon longhouse farms on the moors to seaside villas built by retired captains in Nelson's navy. One of the oldest English building materials, found throughout the West Country, is cob, a mixture of mud, water and wheatstraw. It combines well with thatch.

In recent decades retired immigrants have been augmented by younger moneyed professionals, including architects, artists and restaurateurs. Many whose ancestors have worked the land for generations have left the county.

The county is not dominated by large aristocratic estates, so while very grand houses occasionally come on to the market, it is more common to find manor-sized houses and smaller estates. Farms tend to be small or middle-sized. However, in a large area around Tavistock that was developed by a nineteenth-century Duke of Bedford as a sporting estate there are numerous well-designed and built houses, and the countryside has a distinctively well-managed look.

The Local Education Authority actively encourages diversity and there are over sixty secondary schools, including grant-maintained, grammar and modern comprehensive schools and community colleges, together with twenty-seven private girls' and boys' schools. Two state schools, Collyton Grammar School and Kingsbridge Comprehensive, act as magnets to incomers and thus put up property prices in their areas.

# SOMERSET

*'A mixture of hippies and stag hunts – King Arthur stalks the Levels, Paddy Ashdown yomps around Yeovil and elsewhere persons from Porlock interrupt drug-befuddled poets. The genteel take the waters and Bath buns at music festivals, the rest eat Cheddar and try to avoid the sound of rock from Glastonbury.'*

The varied landscape of Somerset – a much larger county in reality than it might seem on the map – lends very different characters to its several parts. North-west is the wild Exmoor National Park, where even seemingly compatible incomers may arouse suspicion for several generations. The coast by Minehead is occupied by holidaymakers in summer. The Sedgemoor wetlands share the eeriness of Otmoor and the Fens, and turf (or peat) is dug there for fuel. The climate is comparatively mild, but also comparatively damp, with Exmoor having higher rainfall in winter and the Mendips in summer.

West Somerset has one of Britain's highest percentages of retired people. Wells also has a large retired population, a social life that revolves around the cathedral and some good shops. The villages around Taunton, especially Kingston St Mary and North Curry, and Babington between Shepton Mallet and Bath, are currently the fashionable spots. 'A far cry', according to a local observer, 'since the days of Mrs Jennings in Babington, who lived with a hundred clocks, all striking, but not necessarily at the same time.' According to house agents, Wedmore is also popular at present, and the Borough Venture dress shop draws middle-aged ladies from afar.

The new ring road at Glastonbury 'makes it virtually impossible to reach the town centre, and if you do get there you have to run the gauntlet of abusive drunks who sit on the church wall in the High Street.' Nearby Street was created in an arts and crafts manner around Millfield School by the Clark family. Today it draws people as much for the 'Village' discount shopping centre, but there is an all-pervading odour of frying from fast-food outlets.

Road noise is no great problem, since both the motorway and the A303 pass through open countryside. However, if buying in Bridgwater it is as well not to be downwind of British Cellophane.

There are notable public and state schools in Bath and Taunton, and leading state primaries include: High Ham CE, Langport; Enmore CE, Bridgwater; Kingston St Mary, Taunton.

# DORSET

*'Exists only on calendars and chocolate boxes. Naturally the most beautiful bits are the army firing ranges, which are barred to the public. Bournemouth will soon have swallowed the rest.'*

Dorset has suffered dreadfully from Bournemouth swallowing neighbouring Poole, but much of the coast, including Poole Harbour itself, remains spectacular. Bournemouth, characterized as the retirement place for new money, is not generally a town for the young: many people who settle there do not bring their families. West Dorset also has a high proportion of retired people, and the county has a pleasantly old-fashioned style.

Poole and perhaps Weymouth are the westward limits of the Solent in sailing terms. However, the snaky Bournemouth/Poole conurbation which now includes Wimborne Minster as a suburb, is regarded as very other by the rest of this most hierarchical of counties. The Isle of Purbeck is more rugged and wild than much of the county. Inland the physical divisions are between the heaths and marshes of the south-east, the chalk uplands of the centre and the gentle fertile land of rivers and pasture in the west and north-west, blending into south Somerset. Dorchester is one of the smallest county towns, even allowing for the Prince of Wales' Poundbury development.

Socially the chief divide is between west (*the* place to live) and north. A number of very large landowners include the Hon Charlotte Townsend, often described as Britain's richest woman after the queen; also more recent colonies of leading London barristers, actors and artists. The north is generally slower, and it is this aspect of Dorset that has been described as 'a sleepy county, which regards its one to two o'clock hour as sacrosanct'.

The typical indigenous Dorset cottage is thatched with roses round the door – probably built up against a swell of the land for protection against rain and wind. Grander houses may use Dorset flint or Purbeck or Portland stone.

Dorset people are proud that theirs is one of the few remaining counties without a yard of motorway. Thus there is very little background noise from roads. Since the closure of Portland, the most obvious aircraft noise comes from the Yeovilton naval airbase in the north. Generally, there is as little light pollution as noise. Plenty of microclimates include that of Cerne Abbas, which should be investigated by gardeners and people suffering from asthma or allergies. There are subtropical gardens at Abbotsbury, but the coast can be bleak in winter when the western gales are blowing.

The county is good for prep and public schools. The best state primaries include: St Catherine's RC, Wimborne; St Catherine's RC and St Mary's, Bridport; St Augustine's Weymouth; St Mary's RC, Sturminster Newton.

# GLOUCESTERSHIRE

'"A horse! A horse! 'Royal' Gloucester for a horse!" must be the motto of settlers in parts of Gloucestershire and the Cotswolds. If it isn't hunting in "Royal" Gloucestershire, then it's racing at Cheltenham. The latter, of course, is stiff with colonels, while the Cotswolds crawl with trippers. The Forest of Dean is inhabited by ancient coal miners and small boys hoping to become Denis Potter by singing from the tops of trees.'

As well as the divide between hill and valley dwellers there are other obvious divisions: the Cotswolds; the dairy and orchard lands of the centre; the fertile Severn valley, with the major towns; and the Forest of Dean. Cotswold or Bath stone is the principal building material with patches of brick, mostly in towns near nineteenth-century brickworks. Tile and thatch appear occasionally, as at Broad Campden, but roofs are mainly Cotswold stone slate. Non-listed buildings may use good concrete imitations.

Property prices tend to be lower in the Forest, which is less popular with incomers, and the Gloucester/Cheltenham conurbation is now almost continuous. Gloucester Docks are a theme park, but the city retains its commerce, just as Cheltenham remains popular with retired people.

'Royal' Gloucestershire – the Stroud valley from Painswick to Minchinhampton and Tetbury – is as attractive as it is popular and expensive. To the east the ancient market town of Cirencester attracts retired people, but keeps a more youthful persona thanks to the agricultural college. It is close to Kemble and Swindon railway stations, and within convenient reach of Cheltenham, Bath and Oxford. The villages of the Coln valley win both daily and weekly commuters for similar reasons. They are quietly attractive and expensive.

North of the A40 – the area most blessed, or plagued, by mass tourism – there are still large estates, and large houses built by the wool merchants and farmers who made the Cotswolds rich.

The annual air tattoo at RAF Fairford is probably the worst aural nuisance, but only lasts a weekend. The concrete surface of the Swindon–Cirencester–Gloucester link road has proved very noisy. There is considerable pesticide use, and oilseed rape is widely grown. The county is often wet, and if it snows at all seriously – about every six or seven years – the higher Cotswold roads are blocked.

The smartest pre-prep in the north Cotswolds is Kitebrook House near Moreton-in-Marsh, and there are numerous good prep schools, with more in Oxford. Top state primaries include:

Southrep CE and St Lawrence CE, Lechlade; Gretton, St James's CE and Andoversford, Cheltenham; Longney CE and Hartpury, Gloucester; Meysey Hampton CE, Cirencester. There are also excellent schools in Bristol. Recommended comprehensives are at Chipping Campden and Bourton-on-the-Water.

# WILTSHIRE

*'Stiff with standing stones and soldiers. Stonehenge attracts tourists, crackpots and traffic. Later monuments, such as Wilton and Longleat, also breed eccentrics, while Salisbury is heavy with the great and good enjoying music festivals. Salisbury Plain is a bleak blank, but the country does produce good sausages and bacon.'*

North of Salisbury temperatures drop and Salisbury Plain is often snow-covered when the rest of the county, which has an excellent record for sunshine, is not. To the north-west is a limestone and clay area of the Cotswolds, and north-east are the chalk Marlborough Downs. The south-east meets the New Forest; the south-west, along the Dorset and Somerset borders, is woodland. Still largely rural – excepting Swindon there are no sizeable towns – Wiltshire nevertheless has commercial and social centres such as Salisbury and Marlborough, a market town with good shops.

Wiltshire is rich in manors, substantial farmhouses, rectories and good family houses. Northern parts within easy drive of Swindon and Great Bedwyn stations have been extensively colonized by commuters. Swindon has its own circle of dormitory villages, and is part of 'Silicon Valley'. Salisbury society centres on Close and Cathedral. Traffic is a problem, compounded by an inadequate bypass. In some areas of the county social life is influenced by the presence of the army.

The south Wiltshire countryside is based on the river valleys that converge on Salisbury. Despite aircraft noise from Boscombe Down the Woodford valley, along the Avon to the north, is the most expensive area. The Bourne valley to the north-east of Salisbury is best positioned for London, but has 'mixed quality housing'. The relatively sparsely populated Avon valley to the south leads to Hampshire and the New Forest. West are the Ebble valley (secluded, verging on remote) and Nadder valley (on green sandstone and attractively tree-full and hilly). North-west is the attractive Wyllie valley – but 'the A36 takes the edge off it' – with good villages, well populated by serving and retired military.

Army firing ranges and crowded roads around Stonehenge and Avebury at the summer solstice can impinge; and it's best not to live too close to the M4 or A303. The A36 Salisbury to Warminster stretch can be busy with lorries and has a high accident rate.

Timber-frame, red sandstone and slate rather than tile hanging, often with patterns, are all found. Bath stone has a wonderfully creamy look, and is easily worked but weathers as a result – and Wiltshire is a county of extremes.

The best state primaries include: Winterslow CE and Gomelton, Salisbury; Urchfont CE, Devizes; Kennet Valley, Preshute, and Ramsbury, Marlborough; Box Highlands, Corsham; Seagry CE, Chippenham. In Salisbury the best prep schools are the Cathedral School and Chafyn Grove.

# THE HOME COUNTIES

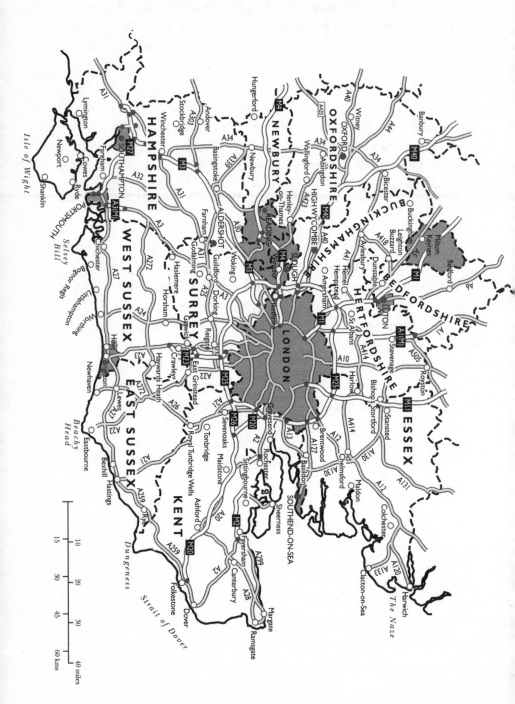

# HAMPSHIRE

*'Thatch and trout are giving way to suburbs and motorways. The county will soon be built over, either by the army or the government, with the exception of the coast which is already an almost continuous development of banal houses for yachties.'*

Soil determines the varied characteristics of different sections of Hampshire. Towards Surrey it is sandy, heathy and covered in pines – in short, good army country. To the west is the chalk that makes the Test such a fine fishing river. In between, around ancient Winchester, is downland, while the old royal hunting preserve of the New Forest is a world, or rather worlds, of its own. The area of the New Forest west of the heath that runs north to south between Fordingbridge and Cadnam and Ringwood and Lyndhurst looks to Bournemouth and Dorset; the villages on the other side turn to Southampton and back into Hampshire. The county has a comparatively high proportion of young people.

Comparatively close to the hub of the London commuting complex, Hampshire generates commuter settlements in areas close to the main road and rail links: Andover, Basingstoke, Winchester, Southampton, Portsmouth, Fleet and Aldershot are examples. However, much of the county is still rural and beautiful with (expensive) 'real village' villages and small towns.

Hampshire is threatened with one of the largest county totals out of the 1,100,000 new homes recommended to the government for South-East England, 140,000 of which are to be built on green belt land or land designated as important for wildlife, landscape or recreational uses. There is also constant pressure from developers for more and more housing projects, which are often incompatible with the existing houses that have evolved organically over centuries.

The county had little good building stone and flint is therefore common, with brick particularly in the north-east. There are even examples of the use of clay and some timber-frames. Slate, thatch and tiles are all common. There are good Georgian and Victorian town houses, and the county is rich in country houses and estates. Modern 'close' and 'estate' houses are often dull by comparison.

The dense network of road and rail links to London, and the consequent levels of commuting, produce a disproportionate amount of noise and vehicle pollution. This can lower prices for buyers. There are also numerous small and medium-sized airports, aerodromes and airfields, such as Blackbush (private and taxi planes), Thruxton (private and racecourse), Odiham (RAF Chinook helicopters), Middle Wallop (army helicopters), Southampton, and Portsmouth (naval flights). No state primaries make the top 500 list – but there is Winchester for later on...

# OXFORDSHIRE

*'Dreaming spires and scholar gypsies vie for attention with the relics of the car-manufacturing industry. The rivers are loud with town and gown failing to punt in a Brideshead-like manner, while Inspector Morse made the area the murder, and beer-swilling, capital of England.'*

As Nicholas Hextall of John D. Wood sees it, Oxfordshire is a quartered orange. Top left from Oxford is *Kind Hearts and Coronets* country. The area top right is farming country. Lower right is Henley, beechwoods, large houses and London-looking. Lower left trickles towards Swindon along the upper Thames valley.

The Thames valley from Goring to Lechlade, an administrative unity since the 1970s merger with north Berkshire, has a character all of its own, and its dampness should be considered by arthritics. Otmoor also retains some of its otherness, not quite destroyed by the extension of the M40. Anyone who watches faces in Oxford will come to recognize the distinctive, rather Germanic, physiognomy of Otmoor farmers. It is known for ice to form on water troughs there in mid-June and, to avoid the

178

butterfly colony in Otmoor's Shabbington wood, the M40 has the sharpest corner on any European motorway.

There are numerous grand houses in the county, sometimes three or four to a modestly sized village. They date from the days when wool was wealth, as do villages to the west, notably Bampton which was once a more important market town than Witney. Despite being the focal point of the blanket industry, Witney itself retains a pleasant centre. Much of the county is still in the keeping of large traditional estates – only Blenheim is the largest of these – some of which have houses to rent. Because of communications, the university, 'Silicon Valley' and educational excellence, any desirable property within reach of Oxford is expensive. The city offers a huge amount of culture and entertainment, but outsiders should be aware that it is difficult for anyone who is not attached to the university to penetrate academic society.

Oxford's morning and evening rush hours, especially on the Banbury and Woodstock roads and the northern bypass, have to be allowed for – generously – by school runners. Noise and nuisance from the M40 is less than might have been expected. The cooling towers of Didcot are as visible from far afield as the nearby prehistoric Wittenham Clumps – provided they are not obscured by their own belching steam. Timber-frame, brick and flint houses with thatch in the east and south, Cotswold stone in the west and many combinations throughout the county echo the architectural prodigality of Oxford itself.

Educational choice, in both the public and private sectors, is one of the many reasons for the recent property boom. The Dragon School, Oxford, is arguably the best school in the country. The best state primaries include: Shenington CE and Wroxton CE, Banbury; Cumnor CE, Oxford; Trinity CE and Valley Road, Henley-on Thames; Aston & Cote CE, Bampton; Crowmarsh Gifford, Wallingford.

# BUCKINGHAMSHIRE

*'The London Underground system used to reach as far as Aylesbury, but withdrew for lack of interest. Since then the county has been largely inhabited by Rothschilds, ducks and, lurking in the Chiltern beechwoods, mysterious bodgers. High Wycombe used to be a continuous traffic jam and was full of East Enders, but no one knows what goes on there since it has been overflown by the M40.'*

As Pevsner noted, there is a greater geological variety to Buckinghamshire than might be imagined, 'with seams of rock giving the impression of a piece of striped (and somewhat ragged) cloth' south-west to north-east. North is the valley of the Great Ouse made up of middle Jurassic sands, clays and thin limestones. One of the last used to provide 'Buckinghamshire marble'. This is separated from Chilterns chalk by thinner bands of gault and various other clays, such as Oxford, Ampthill and Kimmeridge, and more patches of limestone and lower greensand. Several of these manifest themselves in the county's buildings.

Even allowing for the growth of Milton Keynes since he wrote, Pevsner is right in pointing out that architecturally and otherwise Buckinghamshire's character – some strangers might say lack of it, natives might argue for 'characters' – is determined by the absence of a big town, let alone a city. It lacks homogeneity. London exercises its influence from one side, yet the south-west looks to Oxford and the north, perhaps to Birmingham since the extension of the M40.

Buckinghamshire is a county in which great wealth can flourish but need not display itself too publicly, as the Rothschilds understood, and in which a very few miles can take you from the riverside sophistication of Maidenhead to the restrained good breeding of Brill, by way of sprawling High Wycombe and the glorious beechwoods of the secret Chiltern hamlets.

Together with neighbouring Bedfordshire, the county has one

of the highest proportions of people aged fifteen or under in the country.

# SURREY

*'The county's ribbon developments and suburban dormitories are good places to observe stockbrokers and their Tudor. Any other buildings are by Lutyens and Jekyll – except for a few prettified cottages which have survived since the time when Helen Allingham painted them and their jolly-hollyhock-filled gardens.'*

Very much the county for young couples who want to see if they will really like out-of-town living: they can try an approximation of country life without letting go of Nanny London's hand. Physically it is split by the curving M25, with most of the inner section becoming ever more densely populated and suburban. In Surrey terms 'country' begins on the outer side, in the pretty commuter villages. The thin belt north of the M3 – Ascot, Sunninghill and Virginia Water – is no longer either true country or true Surrey, looking as it does to Windsor and London. The other side of the M3, dominated by the army and Woking, Frimley, Farnborough and Aldershot does not have a similar cachet.

Between the A3/A31 and the A24 you'll find many of the most sought-after villages in the south-east as well as the serviceable, and historic, towns of Guildford, Farnham and Dorking. Going from east to west there is a physical and social divide along the Hog's Back, and those who live high on the Hog may look down on the rest in several senses.

There is considerable noise and other pollution from the many motorways and major roads, and Gatwick makes its presence known. Many Heathrow routes also overfly the county. Property prices near Gatwick are affected but, on the other hand, nearby villages are popular with airport staff and aircrew. Light pollution makes it difficult to see stars from many places.

Many of the styles of Kent and Sussex are found in Surrey, but perhaps the farmhouse with clay-tile-hung upper elevations is the most typical. Half-timbered cottages date from the fourteenth to the seventeenth centuries. Bargate stone was much used in Godalming and the surrounding villages, and East Horsley is famous for flint. Above all, this is the county of Lutyens and Jekyll.

In the words of a local estate agent: 'Education is the reason why so many people move to Surrey.' Village schools such as Shere and Puttenham are outstanding, and The Bourne, Farnham, has created its own property miniboom in its catchment area. Other leading state primaries include: South Farnham, Farnham; St Charles Borromeo RC, Weybridge; Burpham, Guildford.

# BEDFORDSHIRE AND HERTFORDSHIRE

*'Bedfordshire makes Norfolk seem hilly, and Hertfordshire is where aspiring Mr Bigs settle if they are not quite in the Essex class. North Hertfordshire people look down on their southern neighbours, but to outsiders the two groups are indistinguishable.'*

Bedfordshire shares with neighbouring Buckinghamshire one of the highest proportions of people aged fifteen or less in the country. However, its birth rate outdoes that of Buckinghamshire, and almost everywhere else. The increase in population, rise in commuting and self-contained new developments in or by villages means it takes time for newcomers to integrate. Too many places have become dormitory villages with no shop or centre of social life – and many commuters prefer to relax by themselves rather than work hard being social at weekends.

There is considerable air and traffic pollution in Hertfordshire, which is not surprising, given the major roads and motorways that run through it, the presence of Luton airport and the closeness of Stansted. Building materials are varied and include clunch (a soft limestone), rendering, colour-washing, knapped flint, a somewhat lavatorial white version of gault brick, thatch, pantiles and pegtiles. Because of the shortage of local materials some 1960s and 1970s developments were unsympathetic, but today's greater insistence on planning should improve matters.

Leading state primaries include: Christ Church CE, Rickmansworth; William Ransom, and Wymondley, Hitchin; South Hill, Hemel Hempstead; St Andrew's CE, Much Hadham; St Dominic RC, Harpenden; Broxbourne CE, Broxbourne; Datchworth, Knebworth; Meldreth, Royston.


# ESSEX

*'The county is known for its strident bottle-blonde girls and Essex man – either a barrow-boy yuppie or a be-shaded and gold medallioned crook. The coast is either industrial waste or irredeemably muddy and punctuated by caravan parks and blowsy resorts like Clacton and Southend. There is also genteel Frinton. Inland all the hedges have been ripped out.'*

Within the inner M25 belt a small area of farms and golf courses survives among the dormitory suburbs and, following railways and major roads, three 'fingers' spread out from this 'palm': from Epping up the M11 by Harlow and Bishop's Stortford; along the A12 to Chelmsford and Colchester; and along the A13 and the Thames estuary to Southend. Between are open arable areas, often denuded of hedgerows, but with charming villages like those along the Colne. The area north and north-west of Colchester is popular with City people, and thus expensive, because access to the station is easy. When the A120, linking the M11 and Stansted to Colchester and the A12, is dualled further areas of north Essex, around the Hedinghams and Finchingfield, will attract commuters.

On the coast, once past the refineries of Canvey Island, and traditional areas of settlement for successful East Enders, all is mud, marsh, seals and wildfowl. Dengie Hundred, the peninsula between the Crouch and the Blackwater, has some commuters. Burnham is its own world, dedicated to sailing. North again are an ill-assorted trio of resorts: Clacton-on-Sea, Walton-on-the-Naze and Frinton-on-Sea – the last a remarkable reservation of gentility.

Areas of west Essex, around Stansted and on either side of the M11, contain many pleasing villages. Pargetting – bold moulded designs on leathery plasterwork – was particularly popular in the seventeenth century. Property tends to be less expensive than across the Hertfordshire border, but the feared blight from Stansted was exaggerated: far from ruining property values, the airport produced a local boom. Its station provides a wonderful commute.

There is constant background noise for a mile or two on either side of the M11 and the A12. Much more obtrusive is light pollution in south Essex from the night-time garishness of the M25. The county has the highest average summer temperatures in Britain, coupled with the lowest rainfall. On the other hand, the east wind must always be taken into consideration.

The best state primaries include: St Peter's CE, West and South Hanningfield and Cold Norton, Chelmsford; Bentley St Paul's CE, Brentwood; Cressing, Braintree; St Thomas More RC and Great Chesterford CE, Saffron Walden; Great Totham CE; Roydon, and St James's CE, Harlow; St Francis RC, Malden; Manuden, Bishop's Stortford.

# SUSSEX

'During spring and summer tourists prevail, roaming villages, towns and Downs. In autumn, however, in the words of a friend recently removed from Wandsworth: "Wind howls and trees are bent, sheep are blown from the Downs. Catholics are hated. Bonfires are lit." This is also the county of shifty Brighton "knockers" wheedling antiques out of old ladies, and memories of adultery.'

Sussex is now divided into East and West Sussex, both of which share many physical characteristics – coastal strip of towns, South Downs, Weald – but are distinct socially. The hills and woods of the East have traditionally been farmed on a smaller scale, thus there are many yeoman's houses, and the distances between villages are not usually great. There are many weekend cottages – and commuters. The West is more open and is still made up of large estates. There are fewer family houses and cottages – and fewer people – and modest small towns rather than the East's many substantial villages. Close to the coast in the East summer temperatures tend to be a little higher than in the West, and inland there is less winter rain. Along the Kent border and the coast the East has a high proportion of retired people. There is a similar patch around Bognor and Littlehampton in West Sussex, which also enjoys some of the shortest dentists' lists in the country.

Sussex owes much to its clay and chalk. Over the centuries the first saved it from spoliation by rendering all but the few post roads to the coast impassable in winter. Sheep prospered on the chalk Downs and, with the Weald's iron and charcoal, made the county rich.

Timber-frame, weatherboarding, Sussex brick, combined flint and brick and tile-hanging – which may consist of glazed and coloured 'mathematical tiles' arranged to look like brick-work – are all used for buildings. The county is the heart of literary England, haunted by the ghosts of E.H. Benson's eccentric dames at Rye, Kipling's Puck, and Hilaire Belloc declaiming over pints of beer.

Aircraft noise is rarely completely avoidable given the increasing traffic to and from Gatwick, and overflying from Heathrow. This is also true of traffic pollution from the various motorways and major roads.

Leading state primaries include: Holy Trinity CE and St John's RC, Horsham; St Thomas's CE, Tunbridge Wells; Plumpton, and Barcombe CE, Lewes; Wivelsfield, Haywards Heath; Stonegate CE, Wadhurst.

# KENT

*'The north coast is mud and power stations; the south coast towns are sinks into which deprived London boroughs pour their problems and the Continent its asylum seekers. In between are hops and orchards, but also towns full of "Disgusteds".'*

There is a world of difference between the outer London suburbs and Thanet or the Romney Marsh. North Kent along the M2 and M20 corridors is first commercial and industrial, then arable. After Maidstone and Chatham there are more large estates, as opposed to the orchards and hop farms of the Weald. The depression the far east of the county suffered with the collapse of coal mining has persisted to some extent, although the 'love drug' effect of Pfizer's operations has perked up the property market around Sandwich. The Isle of Thanet is very much a world apart, and bleak to many tastes. Folkestone has acquired something of a reputation as a dumping ground for the problems of inner London boroughs, but when a high-speed rail link to the Channel tunnel is finally provided conditions will change; and when it is 40 minutes from Ashford to St Pancras property prices will rise considerably for some miles around.

One of the most favoured areas for incomers, especially commuters, is the Weald to the south of Maidstone towards Cranbrook. The roads are not particularly convenient, but the Ashford line is and this is a rich area for reputable prep schools.

The coastal band from Thanet through to Sussex tends to be a little cooler in summer, and inland there can be considerable winter snowfalls. The wettest areas are probably inland on the west, and around Dover. There are seasonal fogs from the Channel and sometimes a danger of flooding in the Weald.

Traditional Kent houses used timber frames often covered with weatherboarding, which was generally painted white or cream unless elm was used, when it was left to age into a delicate silvery grey. Alternatively, protection was provided by hanging tiles: plain, like roofing tiles, or ornamental. There is also a good deal of red brick, at its most attractive when combined with blue headers, and many barn and oast-house conversions, good and bad.

The further east and south you go in Kent, the more rural and self-dependent society becomes and, despite the considerable noise and pollution near the major routes, including the A274 and the A263, to and from the Channel tunnel, there is surprisingly little in large tracts of the county. Dungeness has its nuclear power station. There are a number of small airfields.

Leading state primaries include: Brabourne CE, Ashford; Luddenham, Faversham; Horsmonden, Tonbridge; St Martin's CE, Folkestone; Yalding CE, Maidstone; Chiddingstone CE, Edenbridge; Culverstone Green, Gravesend.

# BERKSHIRE

*'Royalty and horses are the bookends of Berkshire. Windsor at one end, the White Horse and Newbury at the other. Bullion robbers rub shoulders with film folk along the river. For most people this is a county to get through on the way to somewhere else. Those who stop are the geeks and nerds in what passes for England's answer to Silicon Valley.'*

Berkshire has officially been subsumed by the unitary authorities that used to make up Wokingham and Newbury (and the old divisions between the two areas, running south from Reading, is still very sharp). Eastern Berkshire contains much of the most expensive residential property outside London, with Wentworth dubbed the Beverly Hills of England. Because of its proximity to London and Heathrow on one side and 'Silicon Valley' on the other, the area is popular with money, Americans and the international business community. Although protected to some degree by the metropolitan green belt, much of it cannot be considered real country. However, it is notable for its trees and rhododendrons, and there are comparatively unspoiled areas around Englefield Green and Winkfield.

West Berkshire has retained more real countryside, in part because much of it is still owned by large traditional estates. The western downland has also been declared an Area of Outstanding Natural Beauty. In the social sense it is a very desirable area, but the criteria are different to those of the east. Around Newbury the main business is horse, and Hungerford has a remarkable concentration of antique shops. Do not expect too many bargains though: it is regularly fished by metropolitan dealers on a trawl down the A4.

Building materials are very varied and include stone, boulder, ragstone, brick, chalk and flint, with both slate roofs and thatch in abundance. Pale grey brick with red brick dressings is common among early eighteenth-century houses.

Educationally Berkshire has a vast array of fine schools of all types and at all levels. The best state primaries include: Cold Ash, St Mark's CE and St Finian's, Thatcham; St Paul's RC, Englefield CE and St Dominic Saviour RC, Reading; St Francis, Ascot; Chieveley, Newbury.

# ISLE OF WIGHT

*'Either they are mad about sailing, or they hate sailors. The ferries are prohibitively expensive, and in summer the island is overrun with holidaymakers. In winter there is nothing to do.'*

The great determinant of island life is tourism. In summer the population of Yarmouth grows from 1,000 to 10,000 and residents tend to hide away. Shops may well close for the winter, as do many restaurants. Winters are indeed very quiet, and there are high levels of seasonal unemployment. This means that staff wages of any sort are less than on the mainland, although the cost of living is probably higher overall. Petrol and household goods cost more, but traditional skills, such as a mole-catching, often much less than elsewhere.

There is a great culture of dinner and drinks parties, but a reluctance to travel far – there are islanders who have never been to England – means you are likely to see the same people time after time. The grapevine is active: when a friend was thinking of changing her twelve-year-old weekender status for permanent residence, she was told where and when she was moving 'from an impeccable source', before she and her husband had actually decided.

The island has the highest proportion of pensioners in the country. It still has its agriculture, and boasts more manor houses than any other similarly sized area. In property terms, money goes a long way, except for prime Solent-side houses.

East and west are physically separated by the Medina river, but more important is the immense divide between true islanders and overners, yachties and holidaymakers. West Wight is the more rural area and its people are gentler and more laid-back. They tend to regard East Wighters as rather London-ey.

The ferries (Ryde/Portsmouth, Yarmouth/Lymington) are criticized as being the most expensive per mile in the world, but residents now get about one-third off for themselves and cars. If fog stops a ferry – a rare event – it is usually possible to take another from the other end of the island. Air quality is splendid, and a three-minute traffic jam a matter of grave concern.

The island's microclimate – generally about a half a degree warmer than the mainland – encourages numerous subtropical species, and fruits which might flourish in Cornwall but not elsewhere in Britain. The winter fogs are notorious.

Education is excellent. The state system has retained the old three levels: primary, middle (9–13) and secondary. Particularly recommended are Brighston primary school, and Trinity middle school, between Newport and Carisbrooke, which is a church foundation and therefore does not have a catchment area. Other notable state primaries include: Ventnor, Ventnor; Mayfield CE, Ryde.

# EAST ANGLIA

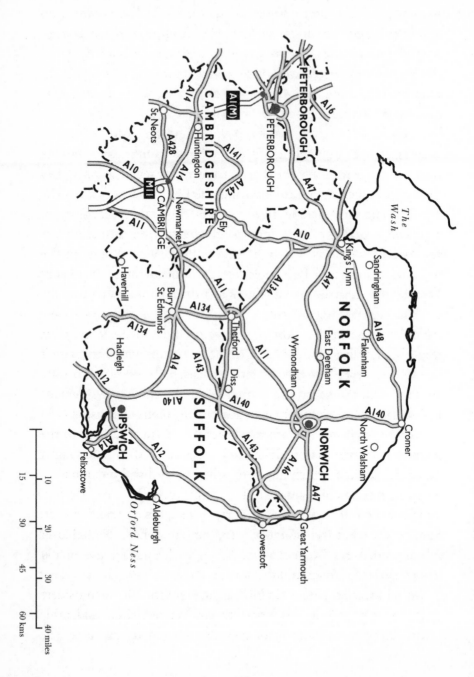

# CAMBRIDGESHIRE AND HUNTINGDON

*'The population of this area is made up of mad academics, web-footed Fenlanders and now geeks. It is very cold and damp, and in winter people warm themselves at the candles of carol services. Rupert Brooke got Cambridge people (who "never smile") and most of the villages right. There never was anything to say about Huntingdon, and there is even less since it lost county status without a whimper.'*

Between 1981 and 1996 the population of Cambridgeshire rose by 19.3 per cent, the fastest growth of any English county, and this is expected to increase during the next twenty years. The reasons for this include not only the obvious attractions of Cambridge and the surrounding countryside, but also the ease with which London can be reached and the proximity of the M11 and Stansted. Unlike Huntingdonshire, the old soke of Peterbrough has freed itself from Cambridge, as a unitary authority. Road and rail communications, as well as the cathedral, make it an attractive centre. The growth in high-technology industry, spearheaded by Microsoft, is another factor in the region's growth but its entrepreneurs face a dilemma: either their efforts to rival California, or even the Thames Silicon Valley, will be emasculated by planning constraints, or their expansion will wreck the environment and amenities that attracted them to the area in the first place. The 1999 planning decision against Wellcome's plans for expansion has highlighted this dilemma.

The area is comparatively far from the sea and mostly flat, which means that weather fronts, once arrived, tend to sit. Summers are hot – this is 'the bread basket of East Anglia' after all – but between November and March there are many, many dull grey days of mist and drizzle.

In Cambridge, as in Oxford, it can be difficult for outsiders to penetrate academic society, although there is a considerable crossover between some academics and the new technocrats. The major division in the county is between the fens to the north of the A14 and the softer, greener, more undulating south. There are very attractive villages to either side along the M11 corridor. To those who live there Fenland is the best place in the world, but it is an acquired taste, and an incomer must be very sure that it is a world to which he or she will be suited.

Leading state primaries include: Park Street CE, Fen Ditton, and Great Wilbraham CE, Cambridge; Bury CE and Brington CE, Huntingdon; Folksworth CE, Peterborough.

# SUFFOLK

'*Silly ("holy", not that you'd know it) Suffolk is divided between Constable Country and Rendell Country, both of which attract pilgrims and clog the lanes. A Suffolk Punch is not something to help take the harm out of the weather, but a large horse.*'

In her *Identity of Suffolk* Celia Jennings showed how local inheritance systems resulted in a county of scattered farmhouses, small manors, often several in one parish, and innumerable substantial properties built by farmers or merchants turned country gentlemen in the late Middle Ages.

West of the A14 is more aboriginal than east, which has seen many more incomers over the last fifteen or so years, reflecting the eighteenth- and nineteenth-century division whereby Suffolk's industry – brewing, corn, agricultural machinery, printing – was largely in Ipswich and the smaller towns in the East. The divide also shows in cricket, the split between Bury culture (literature, music, charity and the cathedral) and the Snape and Aldeburgh set.

The north is generally sleepy with old families and farming, and perhaps 40 per cent lower property prices. Along the coastal strip there is a marked divide between Orford, Aldeburgh and Thorpeness, characterized by golf, yachts, and fortyish City types, and Dunwich, Walberswick and Southwold, where people are less extrovert and rather older. Felixstowe is a Janus town of two natures, with old inhabitants to one side and new around the port. This is one of several places that has been affected by migrations from London. In general Suffolk social life is relaxed, and usually penetrated by incomers via schooling. The east can be cliquey but social cricket is always an introduction.

From the seventeenth century onwards the exterior of a half-timbered house, including the timbers, was coated with lime plaster mixed with hair or cow dung. While this may be washed white, different areas have preferences for pink, ochre or blue. A true Suffolk pink may come as a shock to outsiders. West Suffolk, like Essex, specialized in pargetting. A nineteenth-century favourite was Suffolk gault brick and, especially towards the coast, there are many brick villas, town houses and former railway stations.

A number of state schools create their own mini property markets, most notably Snape Church of England primary; Ipswich School; Northgate Comprehensive; Mills Comprehensive, Framlingham. Leading state primaries include: Stonham Aspal, Stowmarket; Easton, Woodbridge; Chelmondiston CE and Witnesham, Ipswich.

# NORFOLK

*'Very flat, of course, and otherwise full of Broads. The natives may be called "carrot tops" or Swedes but they are essentially Dutch and some still speak an impenetrable dialect like Frisian. They are inordinately proud of the Norwich School of painters and Nelson. They can't afford lobster or asparagus, and so exist on crab, samphire, eels and bloaters.'*

Geographically Norfolk divides into several distinct parts. Around Thetford it is Breckland and forest – one of the largest in

England; there is fen and marsh in the north-west; the Broads are their own world; and in the centre are heaths and great sweeps of agricultural emptiness. Building materials reflect some of the differences. As well as brick there is flint, half-timber construction with plaster render and thatch – naturally Norfolk reed.

The coast of north-west Norfolk is a mass of pale, curving sand dunes, reed marshes and vast, clear horizons edged by pine woods. Much of it is an Area of Outstanding Natural Beauty but in property terms, despite Sandringham, the area closer to the Wash lacks the prestige of the Burnhams, Wells, Walsingham or Cley. However, it has the advantage of propinquity to King's Lynn and the railway. To the south the land blends into the Fens, and to live in fenland takes a particular cast of mind.

North Norfolk, according to a lyrical local estate agent, 'is almost England in miniature. It offers outstanding beauty and diversity, with hills and undulating fields, wooded valleys and forest areas, marshes and sandy beaches.' Like the Broads, the coast, especially towards Sheringham and Cromer in the east, is overrun by holidaymakers in the summer. The seven Burnhams, known collectively to some as 'Chelsea-on-Sea', are immensely popular with sailing Londoners, who flock there in summer. Thus Burnham Market is lavishly provided with antique dealers, butchers, bakers, tailors, grocers, a notable fishmonger, general store, delicatessen, wine shop, a second-hand bookshop, a milliner, an unusually charming bank and the 1996 Pub of the Year. Even those non-sailing locals who prefer not to mix with holidaymakers and weekenders are happy to enjoy the benefits. South Norfolk is largely unspoilt because most intruders pass through to the coast. The area around Thetford is one of those traditionally settled by East Enders.

Twenty years ago Norfolk was notorious as a beer-drinker's hell with village pubs that sold nothing but Watney's. Those days are long past, and there is now as much choice as elsewhere. The products of Suffolk's two principal surviving brewers, Adnam's and Greene King, are to be found in favoured areas and help to keep out the wind and cold. It is, however, a comparatively dry county.

Leading state primaries include: Great Ellingham, Attleborough; Alpington, and Salhouse, Norwich; St Martha's Newlyn RC, King's Lynn; Hillcrest, Downham Market.

# THE EAST MIDLANDS

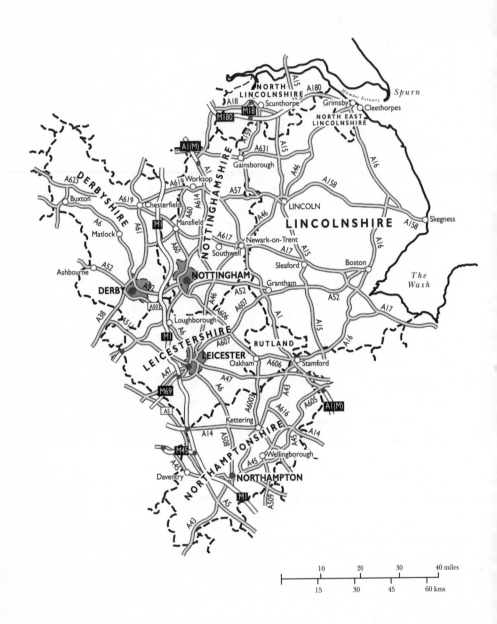

# NORTHAMPTONSHIRE, LEICESTERSHIRE AND RUTLAND

*'The Shires means hunting, and also indigestible pork pies – rightly known as "growlers". Northamptonshire has a drab industrial spine where they make shoes, and there is a church known as "Phipps' fire escape" because it was built by a brewer hoping to escape damnation. Leicestershire is inhabited entirely by hunting folk, but they did manage to pause long enough to invent Stilton.'*

Very grand traditional estates – Spencers at Althorp and Comptons at Castle Ashby, for example – still dominate Northamptonshire and some of them have spawned estate houses which are now very sought after. However, their dominance means there is less of a legacy of middle-sized country houses or large village houses than in the Cotswolds or West Country. The average village has, at best, an old rectory and maybe a manor or one substantial farmhouse.

A stretch of villages along the River Nene turned into small, but not pretty, industrial towns during the nineteenth and earlier twentieth centuries. The industry was principally tanning and the shoe trade. Much prettier areas survive in the south-west between Northampton and Banbury, north of Northampton towards Market Harborough and around Oundle in the north-east.

Up to twenty-five years ago Northamptonshire was a backwater, but as motorways and rail connections improved it was discovered by incomers from London and Midlands cities. It is now growing at much the same pace as Milton Keynes, and attracts large companies looking for distribution centres as well as service companies such as Barclaycard. The people are friendly and incomers soon integrate into the community.

Building materials are mellow, rusty brown ironstone and Cotswold-like limestone. Collyweston slate splits easily into tiles for roofing. Along the Ouse there was good brick clay. All this means that there is no identifiable county style.

If Northampton is one of 'the shires', Leicester is undoubtedly *the* 'shire'. Not every countryman is pro-hunting, but the general enthusiasm for the sport must be taken into consideration by prospective incomers. The county is roughly divided from north to south by the Saor valley. The eastern half, including the Vale of Belvoir, is largely agricultural and bounded by the comparatively high marlstone escarpment. Parts of the southwest, such as Hinkley, bear the scars of old industrialization, and feel the pull of Coventry and Birmingham. There is also a divide in bedrock, and thus scenery and mood, between the harder basement rock in the north of the county, kin to the Pennines and Wales, and the softer strata of the south.

Like Northamptonshire it is a county of great estates, with few farms, rectories or small manors. However, more rural properties are coming on to the market, and there are increasing numbers of barn and outbuilding conversions. Belvoir Castle hosts a number of theatrical, musical and other cultural events. In the east, stone is used for houses. Mud and later brick was used for cottages. There are also many timber-framed buildings, often thatched.

The old county of Rutland has re-emerged from its resented amalgamation with Leicestershire, if only as a unitary authority.

There is a good selection of prep schools. Leading state primaries include: Bitteswell St Mary's CE and Dunton Bassett, Lutterworth; St Winefride's RC, Loughborough; Helmdon, Brackley; Geddington CE, Kettering; Little Harringden, Wellingborough; St Francis RC, Melton Mowbray; Red Hill Field, and Huncote, Leicester; Walgrave, Northampton.

# LINCOLNSHIRE

*'Dickens' phrase in* Bleak House *says it all: "The waters were out in Lincolnshire". It is wild and woldy, with great bleak stretches of arable farm except in the north, where Scunthorpe was until recently the greatest steel-producing town in Britain. The sausages can be good. However, haslet makes haggis sound genteel.'*

The traditional administrative divisions of Lincolnshire still make sense. The largest, Parts of Lindsey, was in the north from the Humber river to Lincoln and then across to halfway down The Wash. It included the Wolds. Much of this division was first yoked, artificially, to Hull and the East Riding and is still separate as Humberside. The distinct North Lincolnshire dialect made famous by Tennyson is nowadays rather more an accent. South-west was Kesteven, and round The Wash to the Norfolk border on the River Nene was Holland.

All three areas have distinct characters. Kesteven, for instance, is a part of 'the shires' and good hunting country and is becoming popular with commuters because it is now possible to reach King's Cross from Grantham in 45 minutes by high-speed train. Stamford, an architectural jewel, and the only complete town in the country to be listed, is commutable from London by the A1 and – just – by rail via Peterborough. It is best known for Burghley House and the horse trials.

Holland, however, is not for commuters, and the area around Spalding and Boston currently produces three-quarters of the broccoli sold by Marks & Spencer. However it is defined, Lincolnshire is reputedly the second largest English county, after Yorkshire, and has the lowest population density so there is plenty of space, and indeed property, for incomers. However, that far away from the commuting areas society is very much dependent on farming communities which tend to be scattered.

Thirty years ago the north of Lincolnshire was very rural, with the obvious exceptions of Scunthorpe, the major steel-producing town in Britain, and Grimsby, the great fishing port of the east coast. Steel, fishing and now agriculture have all declined. In Scunthorpe's glory days the town's motto *Coeli refulgant nostros laboros* (The skies reflect our labours) was a truth at night, but the stars are now visible once more, and there is considerably less industrial pollution. Pesticides could be a problem, as could oilseed rape. Windy and often cold, Lincolnshire has more thunderstorms than anywhere else in England – an average of sixteen a year. The east coast is relatively dry.

The county is well-served educationally at all levels, and is noted for its agricultural colleges as well as for Lincoln University.

# NOTTINGHAMSHIRE AND DERBYSHIRE

*'Everyone knows about Sherwood Forest and its pantomime troupers in fetching green hose. Then there is the great divide represented by the Dukeries and D.H. Lawrence. The Peak is bleak and full of ramblers needing to be rescued and orienteers without a clue where they are. Probably they were heading for Chatsworth, or Bakewell where they call tarts puddings.'*

Nottingham has experienced a considerable regeneration, aided by the presence of two universities, and attracts many major companies including Japanese firms to join the indigenous Boots, Raleigh and Players. This has also given the cultural life of the city a boost, and it is now rated among the top centres in the country for sport, leisure and cultural activities. As a result the surrounding villages, many of which are still largely rural in appearance, have become dormitories for commuters to Nottingham. There are similar villages around Mansfield. Both Nottinghamshire and Derbyshire have survived the collapse of the coal industry, and as new cleaner industries have moved in much of the unemployment has been soaked up.

Both counties are known for the friendliness of their people, and in most rural villages – in particular the very pretty ones in the north and north-east – it is comparatively easy to integrate. Before moving from Southwell to the north of the county a friend made a point of attending the church barbecue, where he was made welcome by people whose families had farmed the area for generations. Land ownership has changed remarkably little in these parts.

The centre of Nottinghamshire around Maplebeck, on the fringes of the Dukeries, is agricultural and hunting country and villages can be remote. The Trent and, even more, the Lincolnshire border are definite social divisions.

Derbyshire, by contrast with some counties to the south, has many very pretty villages which are still real communities, rather than dormitories or uncomfortably expanded small towns. Improved communications mean that south Derbyshire attracts commuters from Birmingham, and this is also seen in parts of the north, where workers from Sheffield and Manchester seek solace in the Peak. In summer the National Park, the Blue John caves and Chatsworth contradict the remoteness.

There is a stark climatic division between the Peak District in the north-west (which can expect serious winter snow) and the southern part of the county, which has half the former's rainfall and an average temperature that is 10°F (5.5°C) higher. Sudden changes of weather – from blistering sun to hailstones and back within minutes – are a feature of the county.

'Keep away from the A1,' advises a local, although he has just moved, happily enough, to a village little more than a mile from it. The north used to be known for pylons and the centre for slag heaps. The latter have gone, and pylons are getting fewer. There is much brick, especially in a characteristic dark plum red but, according to a *Country Life* authority, 'There is no typical Derbyshire village because of the wide variety of landscape and building materials within the county.'

Leading state primaries include: Mellers, St Edmund Campion RC and Toton Bispham Drive, Nottingham; Misson, Doncaster; Charlesworth, Glossop; Muskham, Norwell CE and Flintham, Newark; Primary St Mary & St Martin, and Blyth CE, Worksop.

# THE WEST MIDLANDS

# HEREFORDSHIRE

*'They sweeten their cider unpardonably, and their cathedral and churches attempt to sell off their greatest treasures. Life is very, very quiet – even the cattle have been tempted by pastures elsewhere – but at least you will find something to read over at Hay.'*

Opinions are divided, but many consider Hereford an agreeable city, and it is one of the pillars of the Three Choirs Festival. The country around Leominster to its north is generally considered the most beautiful, and still retains much of its remoteness. To the west rich farmland is overlooked by the Black Mountains, and to the south is the Forest of Dean. Despite the beauty of the scenery along the Wye, Herefordshire is not overburdened with tourists. It is in fact one of the least densely populated areas of England, and suffers less than most from noise and light pollution.

Property reflects traditional social levels in the county: fine country houses for landowners; substantial brick farmhouses surrounded by working outbuildings for tenant farmers; and two-up two-down cottages for labourers. The last were not attractive to begin with and have become less so as they have been extended. A middle class did not develop and neither did 'real villages'. There were, rather, scattered agricultural communities. The few exceptions include black-and-white Weobley and Pembridge, but they are few.

Now that road communications at least have improved, the Hereford-Ross-Wye triangle, the closest to London by either road or rail, is the most sought after in property terms. Hereford – which suffers from traffic, especially at commuting rush hours – is 135 miles (217 kilometres) from central London by way of the A49, the A40 and the M40. Train times, however, are in many cases longer than they were a decade ago.

Herefordshire has countryside that is but an enchanted memory in some other counties. Remember, though, that the Severn and Wye valleys are liable to flooding. Principal building materials are black-and-white half-timbering up to the seventeenth century, and sandstone or brick with slate roofs later. On the whole the northern and southern halves of the county do not mix socially.

Leading state primaries include: St Joseph's CE, Whitchurch CE and Goodrich, Ross-on-Wye; Garway, Hereford; Pembridge CE, Leominster; Eastnor, Ledbury.

# SHROPSHIRE

*'A county that was formerly quiet and modest, but is now the resort of the not quite great and the nearly good, especially in Ludlow. Since Housman and Wodehouse's day it is loud with moping lads and Bertie Wooster's aunts calling from peak to peak. It is often sodden with floods.'*

Shropshire suffers from a certain schizophrenia. The east is dominated by the Birmingham/Wolverhampton conurbation – Bridgnorth has become both smart and expensive as a result – and strongly influenced by the new town of Telford. Particularly attractive to Japanese companies, this now has a planetary system of dormitory villages, and much housing has been provided for middle managers and senior executives. The west has remained remarkably unspoilt and is notable for its many tiny hamlets.

Despite the approach of the M54 Shrewsbury has remained a relatively undeveloped market town, and no neo-Georgian suburbs have sprouted around it. However, even there discreet expansion is beginning. South-west are the sharp hill ranges and long river valleys of Corve Dale, Wenlock Edge, the Clun valley, the Stretton hills and the Long Mynd. North-west small, crowding hills merge with the Welsh uplands across Offa's Dyke, but the rest of the north is generally an undulating plain of rich arable and dairy-farming land – if such a description is still appropriate to any district. With exceptions, it is not as pretty as other parts of the county. However, it too is attracting incomers, many from the South-East – a recent FDPSavills survey of local sales showed that 70 per cent of enquiries came from there. It is a quiet area and possibly not for avid dinner-party goers.

As befits a border county there are numerous castles, some of them habitable, as well as large houses, many of which date from the seventeenth and eighteenth centuries, and estates. There are also quantities of Victorian farmhouses, and a good supply of three-storey Georgian ones. The Severn runs through much of the length of the county, and bridges are comparatively few.

Because of the development of Ironbridge and the surrounding areas during the Industrial Revolution, Shropshire fostered a prosperous middle class of industrialists, merchants and managers who bought land and built good houses. This also encouraged the development of 'real village' villages, with churches, pubs, shops, greens and ponds. It also explains the legacy of Georgian town houses which helps to make Ludlow, for instance, such a civilized town. This tradition of life continues, and there are good restaurants and shops to be found.

The M54 is convenient without causing any problems. The power station at Ironbridge is unsightly, and the attractions of Ironbridge itself must be offset against the numbers of visitors it attracts.

Leading state primaries include: Cleobury Mortimer, Kidderminster; Bicton CE, Shrewsbury.

# WORCESTERSHIRE, WARWICKSHIRE AND STAFFORDSHIRE

'In Worcestershire it is forbidden to listen to any composer but Elgar, or to eat anything without sauce. Other than the bits under Birmingham, Warwickshire is all prettiness and apple blossom, but shudders with charabanc-loads of tourists going to and from

*Stratford. Staffordshire is the Five Towns and grittiness, as chronicled by the unreadable Arnold Bennett. Its inhabitants spend their time copying the pots designed by their ancestors 200 years ago, rather than designing anything new. There is beer, at least.'*

I have grouped these three counties together because they are all to a great extent under the pull of Birmingham and Wolverhampton.

The weight of the industrial West Midlands seems to sit on Worcestershire. Along the M5/A38 corridor there are happy hunting grounds for businessmen in search of country house or cottage. To the west are Stourbridge and Kidderminster. Most towns are east of the Severn with easy access to Birmingham, but there are still many attractive hamlets and villages. The most popular, with many black-and-white period houses and cottages as well as old red-brick houses, are in the Ombersley area.

West of the Severn the countryside is more beautiful. Bewdley is a popular town with fine sixteenth- and seventeenth-century buildings on either side of the river, and Chaddesley Corbett is another typical black-and-white village. Although there is a lack of good period country houses with 20 acres (8 hectares) or more, there are many yeoman farmhouses that have been upgraded to country houses, and many cottages, both black-and-white and Victorian or Edwardian.

Worcestershire is a mixed society of farmers and professional, business and retired people. The last congregate around Malvern, where the views also attract businessmen from Worcester. The city was the birthplace of the Foster Anti-Hunting Bill, and this is a hot subject in the area with passionate pros and antis.

Warwickshire is famously the heart of England. Because of Birmingham and Coventry it is a populous county in the north but the south, which sees the beginnings of the Cotswolds, is still a happy land of farms and market gardens. There are still isolated villages, especially east of Royal Leamington Spa, west of Stratford-upon-Avon and around Shipston on Stour. The romantic Forest of Arden is a district of dense woods and shrub-land. Partly because of the network of major roads and partly because the country is less naturally attractive, the area around Nuneaton and Rugby is less popular. However, communications are good, so the countryside attracts not only Midlands business-men, but also some commuters from London even if they are primarily weekenders.

In Staffordshire there is plenty of good country beyond Birmingham and the Five Towns. The central area is good farm-land, with Cannock Chase to the south and moorland leading to the Pennines and Peak District to the north. Staffordshire clay produced good brick in the eighteenth century. Building materi-als are black-and-white half-timbering in the west, often with thatch on smaller houses; Cotswold stone in the south; ironstone in the south-east; brick in the middle; and sandstone, brick or wood in Stafford.

Anywhere in these three counties it is important to be out of range of the noise of the M5 and the A38, A449 and A456. Kidderminster suffers (seasonally) from a sugar-beet refinery. Be aware that possible town development plans are currently on ice there. Warwick Castle and Stratford generate huge amounts of tourist traffic. So, in Staffordshire, does Alton Towers.

Leading state primaries include: All Saints CE and Oakridge, Stafford; Havergal CE and St Christopher's RC, Wolverhampton; Lapworth CE, Solihul; Dunnington CE, Alcester; St Augustine's RC, Kenilworth; Bridge Town, Stratford-upon-Avon; West Malvern CE, Malvern; Broadheath CE, Worcester.

# THE NORTH

# CHESHIRE

*'The Surrey of north makes Surrey seem sophisticated and glamorous. It is, of course, better known for a mythical cat than for its cheese. Chester claims the oldest horse- and rowing-races in the country, so prepare to lose your shirt.'*

The Wirral is Liverpool's answer to Surrey, while the north of the county serves Manchester in the same way. The south and the Cheshire Plain are still agricultural with small fields, small ponds left by diggers of marl (a natural fertilizer) and dairy farming. To the east is the escarpment and moors of the Peak District. There are still large family estates around Chester itself, notably that of the Duke of Westminster.

The county's architecture was dictated by black-and-white half-timbering until the seventeenth century because its red sandstone was too expensive for general use. Brick was fashionable in the eighteenth century, but in the mid-nineteenth there was a black-and-white revival that later resulted in stockbrokers' Tudor merging with Art Nouveau. Many uninspiring brick farmhouses and the like also date from around the turn of the century.

The M6 is the real dividing line but, like the other major roads, it does not otherwise impinge too greatly on life. Altrincham, Wilmslow, Knutsford, Alderley Edge and down towards Macclesfield and Congleton can be caricatured as the territory of moneyed Manchester ladies who lunch – and caricatures are pointless unless they contain a certain amount of truth. Although it is no longer the case that property in this area is more expensive than anywhere else in the country, barring St George's Hill, it is still very expensive. The controversial new runway at Manchester airport obviously makes itself known to the inhabitants of north Cheshire. Rural Cheshire, to the south and west, centres on Tarporley and there the caricature is of ladies who either farm or play golf but, in either case, certainly hunt. Property in this area, especially around the Beeston and

Peckforton Hills, is increasingly popular. The climate in the county is generally wet and mild: 'We grow good grass in Cheshire'.

The King's School and Queen's School, Chester, are draws. Leading state primaries include St Philip's RC, Stockport.

# LANCASHIRE

*'Lancashire is widely known for* Coronation Street *and the* Beatles, *but can be even more sinister. The south is satanic mills, clogs, cotton mills and docks, relieved only by Blackpool rock and Eccles cakes. Elsewhere seventeenth-century witch trials gave rise to the later passion for coursing hares. Few outsiders can understand Scousers or their quarrels, but Lancastrians are generally cussed.'*

Lancashire is vastly more varied than the traditional stereotype suggests. The south is densely populated, but both Liverpool and Manchester are climbing out of their post-industrial depressions and are notable cultural centres. Nineteenth-century prosperity means that the old mill towns, notably Manchester and Preston, are endowed with impressive civic architecture and art galleries. Lancaster not only has its gallery, but also the Judge's House museum which celebrates the furniture-making firm of Gillow.

History casts mainly benign shadows. The evolution of mill towns as tight communities in river valleys, with owners' and managers' houses on the surrounding slopes, makes it possible to live in glorious countryside within half an hour of several major centres. This makes local commuting easy, and weekend cottages and second homes unnecessary. Another shadow of history is that 'poor, proud Preston', the centre of the county set, and northern parts of Lancashire are still a stronghold of Catholicism. The Wars of the Roses were more a matter for dukes than their counties, but Lancashire's Jacobite history expressed a real religious divide; this persisted into living memory but has now faded.

Physical divisions, marked by a series of river valleys, determine the county's character and these are reflected in its building materials: half-timbering in the south; stone in the north; brick throughout. Perhaps half the county, including most of the built-up areas, lies between the Mersey and the Ribble. Lancashire's coast is not its glory. Several beaches, including Blackpool and Morecambe Bay, failed to achieve the European Union's minimum purity requirements in 1999 despite new sewage works at Fleetwood and Southport.

The central belt, between the Ribble and the Lune, is moorland and undulating hills; tame and agricultural to the west but east – between the M6 and the Pennines – the wild, forested uplands of the Trough of Bowland stretch towards Yorkshire. The Lune valley essentially marks the beginning of the Lake District, and is as beautiful as almost anything there. It is notable for shooting as well as fishing. The fells are much cleaner than a few years ago. However, the mild climate is also very wet.

Leading state primaries include St Michael's Bamford CE, Heywood.

# CUMBRIA

*'You have to be very hearty, since fell-walking and hunting on foot like John Peel are obligatory. At least there is mint cake. It is impossible to drive for crawling tourist coaches and caravans. It is also difficult to escape poets dancing with daffodils and children of all ages in search of Mr Tod and Mrs Tiggy-Winkle. The hills glow with Chernobylized sheep and the coasts with Sellafield.'*

The old counties of Cumberland and Westmorland (not a land west of the moors, but one containing the western meres, or lakes) and the Furness region of North Lancashire were glued together as Cumbria in the 1970s and there are still distinctions between them. The Lake District in what was Cumberland is one of the country's greatest tourist attractions, and is carefully controlled – some might say overcontrolled – by the National Park which can have implications for owners of both domestic properties and businesses. Incomers there include rat-race leavers, who sometimes make the mistake of taking pubs. Few are suited to the life, and many retire hurt. Increasing numbers of high-powered executives also settle in Cumbria although, to generalize, they tend not to play much part in local life.

Lakeland slate is used not only for roofs but also for walls, when it is whitewashed, as is stone. Low pitched roofs, substantial chimneys protected by slate ridges, sturdy porches and dry-stone cow byres under the same roofs as farmhouses are Westmorland characteristics. The weather is mild – except in winter on the high fells – but Cumbria has the highest levels of rainfall in England.

Many European countries tend to become wilder as they approach their northern borders, but Cumbria is half-hearted. Although there is more than a hint at a wild past of border reiving up Liddesdale, on the Solway side all is flat and peaceable. The coast has many traces of its industrial and shipbuilding past, as well as Sellafield, but is still picturesque. What was Westmorland is high and wild, but in the valleys, especially to the south, there are traces of ancient deciduous woodland despite the activities of the Forestry Commission.

Penrith and Carlisle are the main stations, and property prices are higher within reach of them. As a corollary, they are lower in the middle of the rail/M6 corridor around Shap. Sir Richard Branson promises improvements on the west coast line, which is as well since some of the signalling equipment was installed in the nineteenth century. The real environmental problem is neither Sellafield nor old industry, but the immense popularity of the Lake District, which brings coach, motor and foot traffic to the area virtually throughout the year.

Leading state primaries include: Hawkshead, Esthwaite, Ambleside; Hayton CE, Carlisle.

# YORKSHIRE

*'Muck and brass, gritty Sheffield lads doing the full Monty and genteel Harrogate ladies taking tea. Brontës wuther on the heights, winsome vets practise in dales, and Dracula favoured Whitby close to the North Yorkshire Moors – beautiful, but plagued by steam-train spotters. Yorkshire folk take pride in bluntness, spelled rudeness elsewhere. They also have a quixotic affection for losers, from Richard III to King Arthur.'*

True remoteness is still possible. A little while ago I asked Tim Blenkin, an estate agent associated with Knight Frank in Yorkshire, how far away one could still get. He instanced a case in which his journey to view said it all: 'Turn right at the village pub. Drive for three miles over moorland, through a canyon and over a cattle grid. At a barn on the right, turn down a steep single-track road. The house is at the bottom after a quarter of a mile.' In his words, 'This is not just four-wheel-drive country; it is mountain-rescue country. Water comes from the beck, which also powers the generator. There is not another dwelling in sight, and the nearest they get to a crowd is during the grouse season, since this is serious shooting country.'

Yorkshire is now North Yorkshire, the East Riding of Yorkshire and a muddle in the west but this partial reinstatement of the old Ridings – in Old English 'thridings', or thirds – reflects the reality. Despite the confusion of authorities which have turned the West Riding into an administrative patchwork even a deracinated Yorkshireman, such as myself, knows where his ancestral loyalties lie.

Archiepiscopal York long ago lost the status of England's second city, but has its cathedral, university, museum, art gallery and excellent private and public schools. Because of improved rail communications, over the last ten years many businesses have relocated to the city and the flat vale that surrounds it. When a Yorkshireman says York is becoming cosmopolitan, he is referring to this influx of southerners. As a result many of the pleasant nearby villages have seen development, although others survive fairly happily. York itself is a garrison city, and the army plays a strong part in social life.

About 15 miles (25 kilometres) north are the Howardian hills, the 'Cotswolds of the North', where the countryside is generally more appealing and property prices are higher. North again, beyond the A170, are the moors – splendid remote scenery, but not really commutable. East lie the wolds, very pretty and hilly, but rather barren in terms of housing, with large farms and scattered small villages. Towards Ripon lovely old vicarages and village houses are occasionally to be found, in between traditional big estates which have never let their properties go. North Yorkshire regards itself socially as a cut above the west.

Leeds has achieved a remarkable cultural and financial revival in the last few years, and now more than rivals Manchester for vibrancy. To the north it has its Surrey around Ilkley and Bramhope. Holderness in the far south-east is a world of its own, sharing some of the eerie characteristics of the Fens.

The principal building materials are brick in the south and stone in the Howardian hills, dales and moors. The low-lying areas of North Yorkshire, in the lee of the Pennines, are the driest in the North of England. York's average rainfall is only 24.7 inches (63 centimetres) and Hull's is 25 inches (63.5 centimetres). Summer temperatures are high.

Given the numerous cathedrals, minsters and abbeys, ruined and functioning, it is not surprising that there is an excellent tradition of Church of England local authority schools. Leading state primary schools include: Hoylandswaine, Sheffield; Sheriff Hutton, York; Bishop Wilton CE, Sutton-on-the-Forest CE,

Sutton-in-Craven CE, Keighley. The county is also spoilt for choice so far as public schools are concerned.

# DURHAM AND NORTHUMBERLAND

*'Durham life is brass bands and miners' galas – even though there are no mines now. This is Cookson country: fearsome women run businesses, bring up seventeen children and eat stotty cake. The university is old for a redbrick. Northumberland north of the Wall appears to be unpopulated – just a few ruins – but Picts probably lurk in holes beneath the moors. Once-beautiful Newcastle was gutted by Messrs Poulson, Smith and Cunningham. The coastal castles are very fine, but fall down on the job of preventing invasions by weekending Scots.'*

Rugged Teesdale, Weardale and the Pennines, rising to 2,000 feet (610 metres), form the western side of Durham, which falls away eastwards to gentle farmland, common and forest. The coal mining was in the north and south of the county, continuing into south and south-east Northumberland, but recent years have softened the harsh legacy. There is no great variety in building materials. Durham uses brick in the south and east, stone in the north. Northumberland is a county of stone. It is interesting to compare northern stonework with the smoothness of that of Bath or the Cotswolds. Massive blocks, millstone grit in irregular shapes and sizes and large, thick, roof slates may be used.

Durham, Darlington and Teesside all have commuters, as does Newcastle upon Tyne and there is considerable holiday home ownership in the surrounding countryside especially by fishers and golfers from Edinburgh, and also from Newcastle, which scores highly with international (and southern) businessmen on postings because of its amenities and low cost of living. Both Durham and Newcastle have lively student populations, and a good social life.

Not surprisingly this north-eastern part of England attracts outdoor people. It is notable for field sports of all kinds, and Hadrian's Wall attracts walkers as well as historians, artists and archaeologists. Football, rugby and cricket are also popular.

Northumberland, like Durham, has a Pennine belt, and the moors and fells towards the Borders are partly covered by the Kielder forest. Towns and villages tend to be small, old-fashioned and rather huddled. This northern section, between Berwick and the Coquet, is one of England's least populated areas and has huge appeal for lovers of real country. It is quiet from a social point of view, and incomers should be at ease in their own company, but there is some cross-Border socializing. Middle Northumberland is also principally agricultural, but people can look to both the Borders and the Tyne valley. Population is sparse, however, and much driving is needed. Because much of Northumberland is still very much a county of working farms, summers and autumns are marked by agricultural fairs and shows, both large and small. These play an important part in the social as well as commercial life, as do the many garden openings. In the nineteenth century new Newcastle money moved along the Tyne valley as far as Hexham, and many estates still survive. New money now congregates around Ponteland and Darras, where an area is known as Millionaires' Row.

Pollution is slight except in the remaining pockets of heavy industry. The A1, A68 and A69 are the busiest roads, with known accident black spots. The airport might impinge on the Ponteland area. The RAF uses Northumberland for low-flying exercises, and there is often considerable sound of battle from the ranges of the army base at Otterburn. Several beaches failed to meet the European Union's minimum standards for 1999, but the coast is truly spectacular. Winters are generally cold and windy, especially in the exposed central and western uplands, with temperatures several degrees lower than in London. Summers can be warm and beautiful. Rainfall tends to be light in the central and eastern areas and on the coast, but heavier on the Cheviot hills.

Leading state primaries include Staindrop CE, Darlington.

# WALES

If you intend to live in Wales it is important to know where you stand on the language question, especially if you have young children to educate. There is no point in objecting to their being taught in Welsh if you have settled in a Welsh-speaking area. The language is now part of the national school curriculum in most schools in Wales. I consider it enviable to be brought up speaking two languages, whatever they may be. It could be no more than coincidence, but the two best linguists I have met were natives of the bilingual part of Pembrokeshire. One of them taught me French and German at school. As I recall, he spoke sixteen languages, including Urdu but not counting Sanskrit. However, he claimed to be perfect in only eight.

If your children are older and already well into monoglot life, a move to North Wales might prove problematic for them. Nevertheless, one of my informants in the area has had a thoroughly encouraging experience: 'Up here 75 per cent of the population speak Welsh as their first language; the schools operate on a Welsh tuition basis, i.e. unless they are very young, English kids must go and be tutored in Welsh before they can enter into full-time education. My two were dropped in at the deep end and were fluent within a term. If you are not prepared to meet the Welsh halfway (or even a little further) you will have to operate within an English ghetto, which would be a pity. It is worth realizing that our nearest motorway is the Naas road out of Dublin!'

Another friend reports a pertinent euphemism from North Wales. When he asked an intending English migrant if he was going to settle in Anglesey the reply was: 'No, near Colwyn. It's more "metropolitan".' The owners of weekend cottages or second or retirement homes in North Wales no longer have to fear cottage burning, but many of them find it politic to dig up Welsh or, as second best, Irish ancestors.

Wales is often used as a journalistic unit of measurement. 'The size of Wales' means somewhere very small, but distances stretch when you are there and a car journey is likely to take much longer than the map suggests. Planning such journeys is not made easier by the Welsh habit of giving directions by pubs ('Hard left at the Golden Dragon') which may be many, many miles from being local to the speaker.

Since I am not Welsh and have never lived in the Principality, I have relied more than usual on the local knowledge of my informants. For this reason, and because they were such a pleasure to read, I have happily allowed their reports to stray a little from the usual format of the English counties.

# NORTH WALES

*'The land of Druids, or at least oddballs dressed in sheets, ivy and horn-rimmed glasses. Welsh is sung in public, but English is spoken in pubs and shops until an Englishman is observed. Everything is very, very steep.'*

Gwynedd was Caernarvonshire and Meirionydd, and that division still persists. The north of Gwynedd from Conway to the Menai Bridge, is very different from the rest of rural North Wales. The people on this north coastal fringe read the *Liverpool Daily Post*, tune into Granada and have more incomers from Liverpool and the Wirrall. To the west, Bangor is very Welsh. Snowdonia is remote, very rural and also very Welsh, with the holiday cottages of climbers and walkers. Beyond is the Lleyn Peninsula, very popular with the retired – Abersoch is full of 'Wirrall widows' and Criccieth with English – and the sailing fraternity. Pwllheli has a new marina. The nearest large supermarket is near Caernarfon, 40 minutes drive away. Bangor and most towns towards Conway are well served. Meirionydd is full of mountains, sheep, complaining hill farmers, a defunct nuclear power station at Trawfynydd and some excellent hotels.

Clwyd (the eastern part of North Wales) is much more English, and is afflicted by a stretch of caravan-park seaside towns. Social life in the Vale of Clwyd is easier than in

Gwynnedd, where 60-mile (100-kilometre) drives to visit friends are usual. Anglesey faces two ways: Holyhead and Bangor. Llangefni, the county town, has a good art gallery.

The A55 north coast road is the main artery into Gwynedd from England and Ireland. Most of it is dual, but improvement is needed on Anglesey. The A5 approach via Shrewsbury is congested in summer and those in the know take to the hills at Knockin and go over the Berwyns, avoiding Llangollen and Corwen. To strike south you need the A470 – like the curate's egg, good in parts. There are no short journeys, especially in summer.

Only the A55 generates much pollution and aircraft are only a nuisance when the RAF exercises from Anglesey – a much more reliable indication of fair weather than the BBC's forecasts.

Vernacular building materials are granite and slate, and houses look charming if the traditional windows have survived. Gwynedd has some of the finest gardens in the UK, and the National Trust is probably the largest landowner in North Wales.

The only BUPA hospital is in Llandudno, and a 'hospice at home' scheme for the scattered rural population is based in Bangor. There are also cottage hospitals throughout North Wales and an emergency helicopter service. The weather is very varied – Blaenau Ffestiniog is one of the wettest places in Britain, but the mountains are not quite as wet as further south. The Lleyn Peninsula and Anglesey are drier – perhaps 30 inches (76 centimetres) mean annual rainfall, while inland Gwynedd might have 60 inches (152 centimetres). There is a wet and windy time with westerlies from the Atlantic. Snowdonia and Meirionydd are much colder and there is always winter snow.

Educationally, the state sector is good. Ysgol Botwnnog (one of the oldest grammar schools) regularly produces good university entrants. However, the teaching of English at any level can be poor. There are few private schools; Morton Hall, and Hywells are the nearest boarding schools for girls, Shrewsbury and Ellesmere for boys. It might be realistic, given the money, to consider boarding.

# MID WALES AND SOUTH-WEST WALES

*'Sheep and relentless singing are unavoidable, even in Little England beyond Wales. The sheep, of course, could come from anywhere – we have all heard of Taffy. They make a great fuss about their water, presumably to excuse the fact that they couldn't make whiskey, or even whisky.'*

The old counties of Montgomery, Radnor, Brecon, joined as Powys, and Ceredigion, formerly Cardiganshire, make up Mid Wales. Carmarthen and Pembroke, which became Dyfed, are the South-West. The Cambrian mountains run from Glyn Ceiriog through Mid Wales until they plane southwards to the Tywi valley, dividing coastal Ceredigion from inland Powys. Mid Wales is almost entirely rural, but diverse in topography and culture. Ceredigion is now predominantly Welsh-speaking, while Powys is English-speaking – although Welsh is on the increase because of schooling.

Ceredigion, approached by roads through the mountains, has an insular character. The resort and university town of Aberystwyth is home to the National Library of Wales and is the principal administrative centre. Down the coast Aberaeon, New Quay and Cardigan have small, picturesque harbours. Cardigan is at the mouth of the River Teifi which forms a natural boundary with Carmarthenshire all the way to Lampeter – the smallest university town in the United Kingdom – some 30 miles (50 kilometres) north-west. Teifiside is dotted with small farmhouses and the occasional larger country house.

The coast and its small towns, including Aberaeron with its mix of Nash-like squares of stuccoed houses and old-fashioned shops, is popular for retirement and holiday homes. Indeed, most of the small towns in the county have a dated feel to them. The best sandy beaches are at Ynys-las and Borth, north of Aberystwyth. Southwards, the coast is cliffs and small coves such as Llangranog and Mwnt.

Coastal mean temperatures are higher, and hours of sunshine are also high, along the coast, but rainfall is high everywhere, averaging 65–80 inches (165–203 centimetres) a year. Despite the Atlantic, the far Pembroke coast is comparatively dry.

Early Victorian spa towns – Builth Wells, Llanwrtyd Wells and Llandrindnod Wells – are a feature of central Powys. The last, with a population of 4,500, once attracted 80,000 visitors anually and is the administrative capital of Powys. Eastern Powys has impressive castle towns along the Marches. From Chirk in the far north-east down through Welshpool (Powis), Montgomery, Knighton (Knucklas), Hay (of the books), Talgarth and Brecon these small towns developed around Norman strongholds and have an interesting architectural mix.

Houses built before 1800 are more common in Powys than Ceredigion, and often have scarfed crucks, as do farm buildings, some of which were formerly houses. Architecture is generally simple: whitewashed stone rubble walls with slate roofs. There are more sizeable town houses in Aberystwyth, Lampeter and Cardigan. Eastern Powys's building style blends with Herefordshire and Shropshire, and North Powys has many fine half-timbered houses, some medieval.

Both primary and secondary schools are good throughout the area. Notable in the state sector are Pengele Comprehensive, and Aberystwyth. Education in Aberystwyth generally benefits from the university. The independent Christ Church, Brecon, is highly thought of.

# SOUTH WALES

'The coal and much of the industry have gone, so valleys may actually be green, but they are now filled with the sound of cod Dylan Thomas – and the inevitable singing. They used to play rugby.'

The major division is between Monmouthshire and the various

authorities which once constituted old Glamorgan. The former, including the lovely Wye valley and the fringes of the Forest of Dean, is largely unspoilt, a quiet region of hedgerows and untroubled valleys. This tranquillity may seem odd as the area has been disputed between Wales and England for centuries. The coast, between the Severn Bridge and Newport, is flat and very, very muddy. It is also overhung with pylons.

From Newport to Swansea, and inland in the old mining valleys, the legacy of the industrial age is disappearing almost everywhere but those parts which still work, such as the Port Talbot steelworks, may make their presence felt in pollution. However, the greening of the old mining valleys is impressive, and large sums of regenerative money have been pumped in. There are still pockets of unemployment, but no smog and no piles of coal beside the roads. The area has the highest proportion of young people. Although the hospital waiting lists tend to be higher than average, general practitioners' lists are generally shorter.

The quality of the air has improved and is now excellent almost everywhere. There is little nuisance from roads, and very little light pollution except near major conurbations. The RAF naturally uses the Brecon Beacons and the valleys. Wettest Wales is the high region south of Brecon around Merthyr Tydfil with a mean annual rainfall of 80 inches (203 centimetres). However, South Wales now has its vineyards. Overall property prices are rising, and the area is attracting incomers. If they are prepared to be welcomed, the welcome is there.

State primaries are good, as ever in Wales. Outside the cities they are usually village schools with small classes.

# DIRECTORY

## GENERAL

### MAPS

If you have decided upon the area in which you would like to settle, and particularly if you want a property in a country town or a sizeable village, you should get hold of the relevant *Red Book*, or *Red Books*, produced by Estate Publications, Bridewell House, Tenterden, Kent, TN30 6EP (01580 764225), www.estate-publications.co.uk). These are detailed street maps of country towns and the larger villages, and come in three series: Super, County and Local, some of which naturally overlap. They are admirable aids to putting estate agents' brochures in context and can save you time which might otherwise be wasted in visits to unsuitable houses. The Super and Local books are currently priced between £2.50 and £2.99, and the County books between £4.75 and £4.99. Obviously, for still more detailed maps, and many other useful publications, the Ordnance Survey is invaluable (Customer Orders: 01703 792910, fax 01703 792602).

For Londoners a visit to one of Stanford's map and travel bookshops in Long Acre, Regent Street or Grosvenor Gardens will probably be profitable and certainly a pleasure.

Malcolm Hornby: *36 Steps to the Job You Want* is published by Financial Times/Pearson Professional at £13.99. The author can be contacted on malcolm.hornby@malcolmhornby.demon.co.uk

Knight Frank & Rutley's *Buying a Country House – A County Guide to Value*, published in association with *Country Life* (1989). (Unfortunately this is now out of print.)

# WEB SITES

www.countrylife.co.uk
This most important site tells you about *Country Life* and also covers almost every aspect of living in the countryside. It serves as an entry to one of the most extensive nets of useful information for anyone intending to buy a country property.

enquiries@thelondonoffice.co.uk
www.thelondonoffice.co.uk
The London Office, 39 Pall Mall, London SW1
☎ 0207 839 0888

www.foe.co.uk /factorywatch
Friends of the Earth pollution web site

www.propertyfinder.co.uk
Internet Property Finder: umbrella site which saw its total of daily visitors rise from 3,100 to 16,000 in the twelve months to May 1999.

www.upmystreet.com
This site is full of vital local information, including property prices, schooling and crime statistics. You merely enter the post-code that interests you.

# ACQUIRING A PROPERTY

## BUYING AGENTS AND SOURCES OF HOUSE-BUYING ADVICE

**The Association of Relocation Agents**
PO Box 189, Diss, Norfolk IP22 1NS
☎ 08700 737475

**Bircham & Co**
1 Dean Farrar Street, London SW1
☎ 0207 222 8044

**The County Homesearch Company**
The Sight Centre, Newham Quay, Truro, Cornwall TR1 2DP
☎ 01872 223349
headoffice@county-homesearch.co.uk

**The Property Service**
484 Kings Road, London SW10 0LF
☎ 0207 351 6552

**Property Vision**
8 Cromwell Place, London SW7 2JN
☎ 0207 823 8388

**Sclater Property Search**
The Old Farmhouse, Frith, Stalbridge, Sturminster Newton,
Dorset DT10 2SD
☎ 01963 251363

# REMOVAL COMPANIES WITH SPECIAL SKILLS

**Abels Moving Services**
Wimbledon Avenue, Brandon, Suffolk IP27 ONZ
☎ 01953 882666

**Art Move Ltd**
Unit 3, Grant Road, London SW11
☎ 0207 585 1801

**British Association of Removers**
3 Churchill Court, 58 Station Road, North Harrow HA2 7SA
☎ 0208 861 3331

**Cadogan Tate Ltd**
Cadogan House, 23 Acton Lane, Park Royal,
London NW10 7NP
☎ 0208 969 6969

**Hedley's Humpers**
3 St Leonards Road, London NW10 6SX
☎ 0208 965 8733

**Lockson Shipping & Insurance**
29 Broomfield Street, London E14 6BX
☎ 0207 515 8600

**Piano Transport & Storage**
16 Everleigh Street, London N4 3AE
☎ 0207 272 6943

# PLANNING AND LISTING ADVICE

## LISTED BUILDING GUIDES

A *Guide to the Legislation Relating to Listed Buildings*, and A *Guide to the Insurance of Listed Buildings and their Contents* are available from the Chelsea office of Jackson-Stops (0207 589 4536) at £5 each.

## SOURCES OF INFORMATION AND GRANTS

Grant-giving bodies are indicated with an asterisk*.

**Ancient Monuments Society**
2 Church Entry, London EC4V 5HB
☎ 0207 236 3934

**\*Architectural Heritage Fund**
Clareville House, 26–27 Oxendon Street, London SW1Y 4EL
☎ 0207 925 0199

**\*Cadw (Welsh Historic Monuments)**
9th Floor, Brunel House, 2 Fitzalan Road, Cardiff CF2 1UY
☎ 02920 500200
Cadw is the Welsh equivalent of English Heritage, and its historic buildings grants can be more generous than those usual in England. Planning regulations can differ from those in England, so it is imperative to double-check before embarking on anything that may need permission. Similarly the equivalent to English Nature is the CCW, which runs Tir Gofal. This grant aids traditional hill farming, and such environmentally friendly activities as building stone walls and installing decent wooden gates. It also supports measures to lower grazing numbers to sustainable levels.

**Department of Culture, Media and Sport**
2-4 Cockspur Street, London SW1Y 5DH
☎ 0207 211 6200
www.culture.gov.uk

**\*English Heritage**
Fortress House, 23 Saville Row, London W1X 1AB
☎ 0207 973 3434
www.english-heritage.org.uk

**English Historic Towns Forum**
PO Box 22, Bristol BS16 1RZ
☎ 0117 975 0459  Fax: 0117 975 3001

**Georgian Group**
6 Fitzroy Square, London W1P 6DX
☎ 0207 377 1722   Fax: 0207 387 1721

**\*Heritage Lottery Fund and National Heritage Memorial Fund**
7 Holbein Place, London SW1W 8NR
☎ 0207 591 6041

**\*Historic Houses Association**
2 Chester Street, London SW1X 7BB
☎ 0207 259 5688

**National Monuments Record Centre**
Kemble Drive, Swindon, Wiltshire SN2 2GZ
☎ 01793 414600

**The National Trust**
36 Queen Anne's Gate, London SW1H 9AS
☎ 0207 222 9251

**Royal Commission on Ancient & Historic Monuments for Wales**
Crown Building, Plas Crug, Aberystwyth SY23 1NS
☎ 01907 621283   Fax: 01970 627701

**SAVE Britain's Heritage**
70 Cowcross Street, London EC1M 6EJ
☎ 0207 253 3500

**Society for the Protection of Ancient Buildings**
37 Spital Square, London E1 6DQ
☎ 0207 377 1644

**Twentieth Century Society**
70 Cowcross Street, London EC1M 6EJ
☎ 0207 250 3857

**Vernacular Architecture Group**
Ashley, Willows Green, Chelmsford CM3 1QD
☎ 01245 361408

**Victorian Society**
1 Priory Gardens, Bedford Park, London W4 1TT
☎ 0208 994 1019

# RESTORATION AND CONSERVATION

**The Architectural Salvage Index**
c/o Hutton & Rostron, Netley House, Gomshall, Surrey GU5 9QA
☎ 01483 203221   Fax: 01483 202911

**Association of Bronze and Brass Founders**
Heathcote House, 136 Hagley Road, Edgbaston,
Birmingham B16 9PN
☎ 0121 454 4141

**British Aggregate Construction Materials Industries**
**and British Lime Association**
156 Buckingham Palace Road, London SW1 W9TR
☎ 0207 730 8194

**British Artist Blacksmiths Association**
The Old Manse, Kilberry, Tarbert, Argyll PA29 6YD
☎ 01880 770324   Fax: 01880 770324

**British Brick Society Ltd**
c/o Brick Development Association, Woodside House,
Winkfield, Windsor, Berks SL4 2DX
☎ 01344 885651

**British Wood Preserving and Damp-proofing Association**
Building No.6, The Office Village, 4 Romford Road, Stratford,
London E15 4EA
☎ 0208 519 2588

*The Building Conservation Directory*
Published by Cathedral Communications Limited, High Street,
Tisbury, Wiltshire SP3 6HA (01747 871717); £16.95.

*Building Pathology, Principles and Practice*
David S. Watt; published by Blackwell Science.
This newly published book by David Watt is primarily aimed at
surveyors and other professionals but covers much that should be
of wider interest. It is an interdisciplinary approach to the analysis
of defects in buildings and the appropriate remedies. The basis is
common sense: Mr Watt considers how the materials and structure

# Treasure & Son

Treasure & Son, of Temeside, Ludlow, Shropshire SY8 1JW (01584 872161), a firm of master builders, has been passed from father to son for more than 250 years. Stephen Treasure, the present owner, is infectiously enthusiastic. 'It's such fun.' Originally set up in Somerset, the firm – which now has fifty-five employees – moved to Ludlow in 1938. The nondescript façade of its premises belies the astonishing wealth of craftsmanship to be found within – the firm is renowned for its superlative expertise in the renovation, repair and conservation of old and historic buildings.

The scope of work undertaken is illustrated by a list of recent projects, including the rebuilding of part of the outer curtain wall at Ludlow castle; the restoration of a couple of spiral staircases at Warwick castle; and the recreation of the late eighteenth-century decorative plasterwork in St Mary's, Shrewsbury. Current big projects include the restoration of lime kilns on Wenlock Edge, the refurbishing of an eighteenth-century cottage and the making of substantial alterations to a large house for private clients.

The joinery shop is also kept busy working on smaller missions, such as a set of Gothic bookcases. 'It is marvellous to see people's dreams turn into reality, and it is exciting for them to visit the workshop and see the work in progress.'

*Country Life* AMICIA DE MOUBRAY; 6 MAY 1999

---

relate to a building's environment, and how the needs of the occupants and the ways in which it is used give an understanding of its strengths and failings.

*Buildings at Risk* (1998)
Available from English Heritage, Fortress House, 23 Saville Row, London W1X 1AB (0207 973 3434); www.english-heritage.org.uk

**Casting Development Centre**
Arve Church, Birmingham B48 7QB
☎ 0121 454 4141

**The Church Commissioners**
Redundant Churches Division, 1 Millbank, London SW1P 3JZ
☎ 0207 898 1778

**Construction History Society**
c/o Chartered Institute of Building, Englemere, Kings Ride,
Ascot, Berks SL5 8BJ
☎ 01844 346270   Fax: 01844 346270

**Copper Development Association**
224 London Road, St Albans, Herts AL1 1AQ
☎ 01727 731200

**The Council for the Care of Churches**
Fielden House, 13 Little College Street, London SW1P 3SH
☎ 0207 898 1866

**Crafts Council**
44a Pentonville Road, Islington, London N1 9BY
☎ 0207 278 7700
The Crafts Council keeps an invaluable index of leading British
makers in various fields, with slides of their work.

**Dry Stone Walling Association of Great Britain**
c/o YFC Centre, National Agricultural Centre, Stoneleigh Park,
Kenilworth, Warwks CV8 2LG
☎ 0121 378 0493

**Edifice**
14 Doughty Street, London WC1N 2PL
☎ 0207 242 0740   Fax: 0207 430 1672
info@edificephoto.com
This picture library specializes in buildings of all types, from Britain and much of the world. It records periods and styles, materials and architectural and ornamental details and also holds files on architects, gardens and garden features. It is an invaluable resource from which to research restoration projects and possibilities.

**Guild of Architectural Ironmongers**
8 Stepney Green, London E1 3JU
☎ 0207 790 3448

**Guild of Master Craftsmen**
166 High Street, Lewes, East Sussex BN7 1XU
☎ 01273 478449

**Historic Scotland**
Longmore House, Salisbury Place, Edinburgh EH9 1SH
☎ 0131 668 8600

*How to Rescue a Ruin by Setting Up a Local Building Preservation Trust* (1998)
Available from the Architectural Heritage Fund, Clareville House, 26-27 Oxendon Street, London SW1Y 4EL
☎ 0207 925 0199

**Irish Georgian Society**
74 Merrion Square, Dublin 2
☎ 00353 1 676 7053
igs@iol.ie

**Lead Sheet Association**
Hawkwell Business Centre, Maidstone Road, Pembury,
Tunbridge Wells, Kent TN2 4AH
☎ 01892 822773

**Master Carvers Association**
Unit 20, 21 Wren Street, London WC1X 0HF
☎ 0207 278 8759   Fax: 0207 278 8759

**Royal Institute of Chartered Surveyors**
12 Great George Street, Parliament Square, London SW1P 3AD
☎ 0207 222 7000

*Sources of Grants for Building Conservation* (1998)
Published by Cathedral Communications Limited, High Street,
Tisbury, Wiltshire SP3 6HA
☎ 01747 871717

# SECURITY

## GUIDES

*As Safe as Houses*
Available from the Hertfordshire Constabulary, Stanborough
Road, Welwyn Garden City, Herts AL8 6XF
☎ 01707 354200

*Secure by Design*
Contact any Hertfordshire police station

## SOURCES OF INFORMATION

**Salvo**, which is based at Ford Village, Berwick-upon-Tweed TD15
2QG, Northumberland, can be contacted on 01890 820333, by

# Object ID Checklist

This is as useful to owners and insurers as it is to the police.

1   Take photographs. Photographs are of vital importance in identifying and recovering stolen objects. In addition to overall views, take close-ups of inscriptions, markings and any damage or repairs. If possible include a scale or an object of known size, such as a coin, in the image.

2   Type of object. What kind of object is it (e.g., a painting, sculpture, clock, mask)?

3   Materials and techniques. What materials is the object made of (e.g., brass, wood, oil on canvas)? How was it made (e.g., carved, cast, etched)?

4   Measurements. What size and/or weight is the object? Specify which unit of measurement is being used (e.g., centimetres or inches) and to which dimension the measurement refers (e.g., height, width, depth – this is the conventional order among cataloguers).

5   Inscriptions and markings. Are there any identifying markings, numbers or inscriptions on the object (e.g., a signature, dedication, title, maker's marks, purity marks, property marks)?

6   Distinguishing features. Does the object have any physical characteristics that could help to identify it (e.g., damage, repairs or manufacturing defects)?

7   Title. Does the object have a title by which it is known and might be identified (e.g., *The Scream*)?

8   Subjects. What is being pictured or represented (e.g., landscape, battle, woman holding child)?

9   Date or period. When was the object made (e.g., 1893; early seventeenth century; late Bronze Age)?

10  Maker. Do you know who made the object? This may be the name of a known individual (e.g., Thomas Tompion), a company (e.g., Tiffany) or a cultural group (e.g., Hopi).

> 11  Write a short description. This can include any additional informa-
> tion which helps to identify the object (e.g., colour and shape,
> where it was made).
> 12  Keep it secure. Having documented the object, keep the informa-
> tion in a secure place.
> Information about the Council for the Prevention of Art Theft (CoPat) is
> on **www.copat.freeserve.co.uk**, address CoPat, 17 Whitcomb Street,
> London WC2H 7PL. More details of Object ID are on the Getty
> Information Institute's site: **//www.gii.getty.edu**

fax on 01890 820499 or by email: salvo@salvo.co.uk. Their web site, which has dealers' lists, a register of recommended crafts-men, details of auctions and much useful advice, is www.salvo.co.uk

**Thesaurus – ACTS**
Mill Court, Furlongs, Newport, Isle of Wight PO30 2AA
☎ 01983 826000
The Thesaurus Active Crime Tracking System is the world's largest fully searchable database of stolen art and antiques.

# PROTECTIVE MEASURES

**Identidot**
Milford House, 260 Lichfield Road, Mere Green,
Sutton Coldfield B74 2UH
☎ 0121 250 2250
www.Identidot.com/

**SmartWater**
Unit 3, Abbotts Quay, Monks Ferry, Birkenhead,
Merseyside CH41 5LH
☎ 0151 6470700

**Country Watch and FarmWatch**
PC Peter Hale, Thames Valley Police Station,
Marlborough Street, Faringdon, Oxfordshire, SN7 7JP
☎ 01367 244223   Fax: 01235 776092

# INSURANCE

**Axa Nordstern Art Insurance Ltd**
78 Leadenhall Street, London EC3A 3DH
☎ 0207 626 5001
Clare Pary, an underwriter with this company, tells me that, 'Over
95 per cent of our clients have good security. We talk over their
way of life and how best to adapt security to it. Access to a large
country house within an estate can be very open. There may be
three or four entrance gates left open at night when they should
be locked and monitored. We like farmworkers, active game-
keepers and others to be given a security role, and the local fire
brigade to be involved.

'For the more modest house, external lights and CCTV are
recommended, as well as securing any garden statues and ornaments, usually by drilling bolts into plinths.'

**Chubb Insurance Company of Europe**
106 Fenchurch Street, London EC3 M5NB
☎ 0207 867 5555

**Gauntlet Insurance Services**
Wigglesworth House, Southwark Bridge Road, London SE1 9HH
☎ 0207 394 2400
Gauntlet Classic policy for 'fine town and country houses'
includes: cover of fine art, antiques and jewellery, with accidental
damage and depreciation automatically included; an additional
15 per cent of the building sum insured for no extra premium to
cover architect's and surveyor's fees; cover for personal money,

freezer contents and pedal cycles at no extra cost; domestic legal requirements; and interest on any agreed claim over £2,500 which remains unpaid for more than four working days.

**Hiscox plc**
1 Great St Helen's, London EC3A 6HX
☎ 0207 448 6000
www.hiscox.com
Hiscox is a company that has its own art collection, and it is thus sensitive to the needs of collectors. As well as handling insurance for yachts, private aircraft, political risk, kidnap and ransom, it covers high-value homes and has specialized fine art insurance for private collectors. Some of the benefits are: an agreed value on listed items; physical loss or damage can be covered worldwide, including transit risks; new acquisitions are included up to 10 per cent of the aggregate value listed – these should be notified within 60 days of purchase; in the event of theft you have the option to repurchase recovered property; and rapid settlement of claims with interest on claims over $2,500 received within ten working days.

**Tolson Messenger**
148 King Street, London W6 0QU
☎ 0800 374246
www.tolsonmessenger.co.uk
This company has a special Home-Business Insurance policy covering computers and electronic equipment for people working from home. They also insure stock and portable equipment such as laptops and phones, as well as covering business liability and interruption.


# VALUERS

**Gurr Johns**
16 Pall Mall, London SW1Y 5NB
☎ 0207 670 1111

**Weller King**
36 High Street, Steyning, West Sussex BN44 3YE
☎ 01903 816633
Specialist fine art valuers and agents.

**Wellington Personal Insurances**
88 Leadenhall Street, London EC3A 3BA
☎ 0207 929 2811

# WORKING OR RUNNING A BUSINESS FROM HOME

## BUSINESS BACK-UP – WEB SITES

www.ownbase.org.uk
OwnBase, Birchwood, Hill Road South, Helsby,
Cheshire WA6 9PT.

www.better-business.co.uk
Cribau Mill, Llanvair Discoed, Chepstow NP16 6RD
☎ 01291 641 222
Publishes *Better Business* for the self-employed; closely
involved with the web-site designer Siserone, PO Box 103, Reading
RG4 6Y6
☎ 0118 954 5143

www.hba.org.uk
Home Business Alliance, The Firs, High Street, March,
Cambridgeshire PE15 9LQ
☎ 01945 463303

## OTHER USEFUL SOURCES
## OF SPECIALIST ADVICE

| | |
|---|---|
| British Chamber of Commerce | 0207 565 2000 |
| Blind In Business | 0207 588 1885 |
| British Franchising Association | 01491 578 049 |
| British Venture Capital Association | 0207 240 3846 |
| Business Clubs UK | 01709 570400 |
| Business Links | 0345 567 765 |
| Companies House | 02920 380 801 |
| Consumers Association | 0207 486 5544 |
| Crafts Council | 0207 278 7700 |
| Dept of Education and Employment | 0207 925 5000 |
| Department of Trade and Industry | 0207 215 5000 |
| Direct Marketing Association | 0207 321 2525 |
| Direct Selling Association | 0207 497 1234 |
| Forum of Private Businesses | 01565 634 467 |
| HM Customs and Excise | 01702 348 944 |
| Independent Banking Advisory Service | 01487 843 444 |
| Institute of Export | 0207 247 9812 |
| Institute of Management | 01536 204 222 |
| Lawyers for Your Business | 0207 405 9075 |
| Livewire | 0191 261 5584 |
| Mail Order Traders Association | 01704 563787 |
| National Association of Citizens' Advice Bureaux | 0207 833 2181 |
| Office of Fair Trading | 0845 722 4499 |
| Prince's Youth Business Trust | 0800 842 842 |
| Rural Development Commission | 01722 336 255 |
| TEC National Council | 0207 735 0010 |

The Institute of Management publishes checklists including *Running a Small Business from Home* (0207 497 0496).

# GARDENS

## RESEARCH AND ADVICE

**British Archaeology Association
and Royal Archaeological Institute**
c/o Society of Antiquaries of London, Burlington House,
Piccadilly, London W1V OHS
☎ 0207 734 0193

**Council for British Archaeology**
Bowes Morrell House, 111 Walmgate, Yorkshire Y01 9WA
☎ 0190 467 1417

**Garden History Society**
70 Cowcross Street, London EC1M 6EJ
☎ 01432 354479

**Henry Doubleday Research Association**
Ryton Organic Gardens, Coventry CV8 3LG
☎ 024 7630 3517

**Historic Farm Buildings Group**
c/o Museum of English Rural Life, University of Reading,
Whiteknights, P.O.Box 229, Reading, Berks RG6 6AG
☎ 0118 931 8660

**National Vegetable Society**
Secretary: Mr. L.Cox, 33 Newmarket Road, Cleveland TS10 2HY
☎ 01642 484470

*Ponds and Water Gardens*
by Bill Heritage (Blandford Press, 1981, revised 1986)
This is still one of the best books on the subject.

**Royal Horticultural Society**
PO Box 313, London SW1P 2PE
☎ 0207 834 4333

# The Soil Association

The Soil Association was founded in 1946, and is a membership charity which promotes organic food and farming. It is at the centre of the campaign for safe, healthy food, an unpolluted countryside and a sustainable, organic farming policy in Britain and worldwide. Now one of the United Kingdom's top 500 charities, it has 15,000 members and supporters. Key areas of work include:

◆ Consumer campaigns and information on organic food, farming, health, nutrition and the environment.

◆ Local food links which promote direct links between producers and consumers to develop a network of local, affordable organic food marketing schemes, including box schemes, farmers' markets, etc.

◆ Advice and support to organic farmers through the producer services division, with the aim of developing the organic market. A wide range of technical and marketing information is available to producers through guides, events, and seminars and a quarterly journal. The Soil Association also provides help and advice to new entrants through the Organic Conversion Information Service which is funded by the Ministry of Agriculture, Fisheries and Food.

◆ Soil Association Standards for Organic Food and Farming have been developed over a period of twenty-five years and now form the basis of the universally accepted Soil Association Symbol awarded to certified producers and retailers. Soil Association Certification Ltd, a subsidiary company, runs the certification scheme which is used by 70 per cent of the United Kingdom's organic industry.

# FARMLAND AND FARMING

**Country Landowners' Association**
16 Belgrave Square, London SW1X 8PQ
☎ 0207 235 0511

**Ministry of Agriculture, Fisheries and Food**
Nobel House, 17 Smith Square, London SW1P 3JR
www.maff.gov.uk

**National Farmers Union**
164 Shaftesbury Avenue, London WC2H 8HL
☎ 0207 331 7200
www.nfu.org.uk

**Rural Development Commission**
141 Castle Street, Salisbury, Wilts SP1 3TP
☎ 01722 336255

**Soil Association**
Bristol House, 40-56 Victoria Street, Bristol BS1 6BY
☎ 0117 929 0661
www.soilassociation.org
This key web site for those interested in organic food and farming
provides up-to-date lists of farmers' markets as well as details of
research papers, campaigns and current concerns.

# TRANSPORT

## WEB SITES *Research by Jodi Lawson*

www.pti.org.uk
This is the key for Internet information on public transport in the

United Kingdom. It covers all modes of travel, and the pages are organized as follows:

**Express coach travel:** This details the services offered by National Express and Scottish Citylink, which between them cover the United Kingdom. It enables you to map out your route and find out about prices.

**Rail travel:** This provides:
1 Rail timetables online with a link to the official National Rail Journey Planner site provided by Railtrack.
2 The train-line train-time finder, showing available trains at given times between stations of your choice, with prices, journey times and changes.
3 Weekend rail travel news.
4 The official site of Northern Ireland Railways.
5 Brit Rail International, the official site of the specialist ticket and travel agency aimed principally at people seeking information from outside the United Kingdom. It has information on rail travel on the Continent as well as within Britain.
6 Britain by Brit Rail specializes in bookings, rail passes and travel within the United Kingdom.
7 Rail Travel Services enable you to buy advance tickets on the Web.
8 United Kingdom train tickets is a service for purchasing rail tickets by telephone.

**Ferry travel**

**National phone hotline:** This provides the numbers you might need when planning a journey to a particular destination.
1 Journey Call (0906 5500 000) can be called only from within the United Kingdom. It has details of all rail, bus and coach travel. Premium rate phone charges. Operator service costs £1.00 a minute.

2    National Rail Enquiry Service (0345 48 49 50) gives rail information for the United Kingdom, except for Heritage Railways. It is a twenty-four hour service and charges at local rates.

3    National Express Coach Enquiry Service (0990 80 80 80) charges at national rates.

4    Tripscope (08457 585 641) is an important helpline for elderly and disabled people. It gives specialist advice on most aspects of transport, whatever the disability.

**Leisure trips by public transport:** This has links to sites with details of public transport trips such as the National Trust's 'Explorer Britain' hop on-hop off coach tour of Britain, or the 'Guide Friday' hop on-hop off scenic tour of historic towns.

**Major travel groups:** This links to the official sites of the various groups, including those listed below, and provides a huge amount of information not only on timetables, routes, etc., but sometimes also on the company itself.

◆    Arriva bus service covers the North-West, North Wales, Shropshire, North Midlands, Shires, North-East, Northumbria and Yorkshire as well as certain London routes.

◆    BAA operates all the major British airports and will provide details of air travel.

◆    Eurotunnel's official site has timetables for the various destinations and links.

◆    First Group is both a rail and bus company and also has interests in airports. Its buses operate in Yorkshire, Lancashire, the East and West Midlands, East Anglia, the South-East, South-West and Wales.

◆    Go Ahead bus company covers London, Oxford, Buckinghamshire, Brighton and the North-East.

◆    P & O provides details of ferry services.

◆    Prism Rail runs train services in Wales and the South-West and in parts of East Anglia.

◆ Railtrack's site should provide information on future plans as well as present realities.
◆ Stagecoach Holdings cover a great deal of England and Scotland.
◆ Stena Line provides information about ferries.
◆ Virgin Group operates west coast trains from London and Midland trains from Birmingham.
◆ Vivendi, a French company, has many interests around the world, among them a share of the Connex rail services.

The following web sites offer excellent up-to-date information and enable you to book online:

www.kentell.demon.co.uk/indexhtml
British Bus Web Page

www.busweb.co.uk
www.newstide.com/ukbus/index.html
Busweb

# COUNTRY CONCERNS

**The Council for the Preservation of Rural England**
Warwick House, 25 Buckingham Palace Road,
London SW1W 0PP
☎ 0207 976 6433
www.greenchannel.com

**The Countryside Agency**
John Dower House, Crescent Place, Cheltenham,
Gloucestershire GL50 3RA
☎ 01242 521381
www.countryside.gov.uk

# The Village Rural Services Association

Together with the church, school and pub, the shop and the post office have always been a focal point for village life. During the past twenty years, however, many rural areas have lost this hub and too late discovered how important it was to the community's well-being. So the judges of the 1999 Country Life Awards had little difficulty in commending the Village Rural Services Association for its efforts to help small rural communities retain and revive their shops and post offices.

Founded in 1992 and an educational charitable trust since 1997, ViSRA offers an unique blend of advice, training, contacts and encouragement at ground level. It is not self-financing but relies on individuals and organizations to provide funds.

**Countryside Alliance**
The Old Town Hall, 367 Kennington Road, London SE11 4PT
☎ 0207 582 5432
info@countryside-alliance.org
www.countryside-alliance.org

**The Village Rural Services Association**
The Little Keep, Bridport Road, Dorchester, Dorset DT1 1SQ
☎ 01305 259383
www.village-shop.com/virsa
The main focus of ViRSA is supporting sole shops in communities of 1,500 inhabitants or less, but Peter Jones, its founder, emphasizes that it does not confine itself to this shops but also encourages and enables people to take over and run other necessities, such as pubs and garages.

# SOURCES OF HORSEKEEPING ADVICE

**The Pony Club**
NAC Stoneleigh Park, Kenilworth, Warwickshire CV8 2RW
☎ 01203 698 300
www.pony-club.org.uk
Among the club's many useful publications, there is one that is essential reading for adult beginners as well as children: *The Manual of Horsemanship*, £12.50, which is now in its eleventh, thoroughly updated, edition.

**J. Allen and Company**
4 Lower Grosvenor Place, London SW1W 0EL
☎ 0207 834 5606
Specialist booksellers

# SOURCES OF RAMBLING ADVICE

**The Countryside Rights Association**
Freepost ANG 6581, Sandy, Bedfordshire SG19 3YA
☎ 01375 892892

**The Ramblers' Association**
1/5 Wandsworth Road, London SW8 2XX
☎ 0207 339 8500
ramblers@london.ramblers.org.uk

**The Ramblers' Association, Wales**
Ty'r Cerddwyr, High Street, Gresford, Wrexham,
Clwyd LL12 8PT
☎ 01978 855148
cerddwyr@wales.ramblers.org.uk

# INDEX